The
Beverly Lewis
Amish Heritage
COOKBOOK

By Beverly Lewis

*with David Lewis

04C

The
Beverly Lewis
Amish Heritage
COOKBOOK

BETHANYHOUSE
PUBLISHERS
MINNEAPOLIS, MINNESOTA

The Beverly Lewis Amish Heritage Cookbook
Copyright © 2004
Beverly Lewis

Cover design and photography by Dan Thornberg
Interior design by Jennifer Parker
Interior illustrations by Jennifer Horton
Back cover photo by Daryl Martin/Gene Photography

Scripture quotations are from the King James Version of the Bible.

Grateful acknowledgment is given for permission to reprint the following items:
    Songs of the Ausbund, the English translation of *O Gott Vater*, from *Das Lob Lied*—
"Song of Praise," copyright 1998. Reprinted by permission of the Ohio Amish Library,
Millersburg, Ohio. Contact Ohio Amish Library, Inc., 4292 SR 39, Millersburg, OH 44654
to order *Songs of the Ausbund (History and Translations of Ausbund Hymns)*.
    "New Mercies" by Alice Reynolds Flower, from *Along a Gentle Stream*, copyright 1987,
Gospel Publishing House, Springfield, Missouri. Used with permission.
    Date Pudding, Chocolate Peanut Butter Frosting, Katie Fisher's Beef Stew, Broccoli and
Cauliflower Salad, Salad Dressing, Grape Mush Dessert, Baby Pearl Tapioca, Cauliflower
and Broccoli Soup from *Katie's Kitchen*, by Katie S. Fisher of Lancaster County,
Pennsylvania. To order her Amish cookbook, write to: Emmanuel and Katie Fisher, 338
N. Ronks Road, Bird-in-Hand, Pennsylvania 17505.

Published by Bethany House Publishers
11400 Hampshire Avenue South
Bloomington, Minnesota 55438

Bethany House Publishers is a division of
Baker Publishing Group, Grand Rapids, Michigan.

Printed in the United States of America

Library of Congress Cataloging-in-Publication Data

Lewis, Beverly, date
    The Beverly Lewis Amish heritage cookbook : over 200 favorite time-tested recipes / by
Beverly Lewis.
        p. cm.
    Includes index.
    ISBN 0-7642-2917-6 (comb-bound : alk. paper)
    1. Cookery, Amish. I. Title.

    TX715.L6673   2004
    641.5'66   dc22   2004002182

Dedication

To Priscilla Stoltzfus,
wonderful-good friend.

Christian Aid Ministries of Berlin, Ohio, is the recipient of the author royalty earnings from *The Beverly Lewis Amish Heritage Cookbook*. CAM's specific endeavors include distribution of food, clothing, and medical supplies for the needy in Eastern Europe, Liberia, Haiti, and Nicaragua, as well as aid for orphanages in both Romania and Liberia.

Acknowledgments

To the superb (and generous) cooks who shared family recipes or helped in a variety of ways less visible, I am sincerely grateful. They are the following contributors:

Fay Landis, Ruth Mellinger, Darlene Smoker, Rhoda Dombach, Irene Nolt, Mary Jane Hoober, Dorothy Brosey, Julie Buxman, Priscilla Stoltzfus, Leon and Joyce Hershey, Cherie Lynn Hershey, Aleta Hirschberg, Iris Jones, Judy Verhage, Sharon Johnson, Cheryl Ann Clow, Glenda Cooper, Cheryl Zimlich, Omar and Dorothy Buchwalter, Barbara Birch, Jane Buchwalter Jones, John and Ada Reba Bachman, Verna Flower, Katie S. Fisher, Sarah Ebersol, Susie Stoltzfus, Geraldine (Gerry) Goshert, Emma Ebersol, Diana Horgen, Denise Kerr, Hank Hershberger, Dale Gehris, Joyce Eby, and David Lewis.

My splendid editors, Carol Johnson, Julie Smith, and Cheri Hanson, made the editorial process seem nearly effortless. My heartfelt thanks!

Contents

A Personal Glimpse

ADA BUCHWALTER
1886–1954

My maternal grandmother, Ada Groff (Ranck) Buchwalter, was the youngest of five children, born to Amos and Barbara Ranck of Strasburg, Pennsylvania. They were farmers and devout Old Order Mennonites.

During her teen years Ada was courted by a handsome young man with chestnut hair and blue eyes—Omar Neff Buchwalter, who lived with his Mennonite family across the narrow road that in those days divided the villages of Strasburg and Paradise. Sometimes as Ada set about doing her daily farm chores, her cheerful whistling reached Omar's ears. (The name *Ada* means *joyful* in German.)

When Ada told her parents of her engagement to Omar (who was more interested in preaching than farming, and who by now had attended one year as a ministerial student at non-Mennonite Nyack Bible Institute in New York), Ada's father was strongly opposed to the couple's plans. Nevertheless, Omar and Ada were wed on September 13, 1906, and Ada and her new husband were no longer welcome in her family home. (My first novel, *The Shunning*, is loosely based on Ada's life.)

Yet my grandmother, young as she was, drew strength and courage from God. Her life was a testament of grace, and her quiet and gentle spirit influenced each of her eight children, including my mother, Jane. Many of Ada's offspring—children, grandchildren, and great-grandchildren—have been involved in Christian ministry at home and abroad. (Daughter Beulah is buried in Ghana, West Africa, having died as a young missionary while writing a Bible primer in a tribal language.)

As a minister's wife, Ada's gift of warm hospitality meant offering her "wonderful-good" cooking and cozy bedrooms to a steady stream of American pastors and British missionaries, including Smith Wigglesworth, a faith healer and evangelist of the early 1900s. This was during the Great Depression, yet my grandparents happily opened their home and hearth to many. Ada Buchwalter went home to her heavenly reward on June 14, 1954.

I am truly indebted to my grandmother for her shining example—as well as for the wealth of recipes she has passed on to the family . . . and now to you, my loyal readers!

Letter to Readers

My Dear Reader,

Happy cooking and baking!

If you have already read my comments about Ada Buchwalter, my grandmother, you can imagine the joy and near childlike wonder I experienced when my dear mother offered Ada's old wooden recipe box to me last year! For weeks I simply cherished it, looking at it fondly on my dresser where it sat—front and center. I found myself hesitant to even open the lid and investigate the many handwritten recipes I knew were tucked inside.

When I did sit quietly reading each faded recipe card, I felt as if I had been given a heartwarming glimpse into the past. Some months later I decided—with the enthusiasm and encouragement of my publisher, Gary Johnson, and my editor, Carol Johnson—that these wonderful old recipes must see the light of day yet again and be joyfully shared with you. Not only do they come from the hand of master cook and baker Grandmother Ada, but I, along with my tireless helpers, have taken great care to test these delicious dishes, along with oodles of Amish recipes and other scrumptious dishes unique to the Plain community, much to the delight of my own immediate and extended family.

Included are kitchen hints and tips, as well as Amish lore, poetry, and pertinent Scriptures, favorites of the Plain people. Also scattered throughout, you'll find personal notes from me to you . . . hopefully helpful comments, as well as family anecdotes and warm memories of bygone days.

In addition, certain recipes have been modified or updated from the Old Order way of doing things (such as cooking on woodstoves and beating batter by hand—and feeling or tasting one's way through a recipe instead of jotting it down) for the benefit of non-Amish cooks who may have less time to spend in the kitchen. If you find yourself wondering about various ingredients listed, please know that present-day Amish *do* go to the store; they don't necessarily cook *everything* "from scratch."

Truly, this cookbook would not have been possible without the help of my wonderful daughter Julie and my dear cousins Joyce and Cherie Lynn Hershey, who cheerfully kitchen-tested and/or typed endless recipes.

Joyfully yours,

Beverly

Appetizers and Beverages

Mary Ruth hurried with Hannah to help Mamma, Leah, and Lizzie with a smorgasbord-style spread laid out on long tables in the sunny kitchen. Today being a perfect day for a picnic, the People would eat and fellowship on the grounds. Bread and homemade butter, sliced cheeses, dill and sweet pickles, strawberry jam, red beets, half-moon apple pies, and ice-cold lemonade—the standard light fare for a summer Sunday go-to-meeting. Not that a body could eat himself full on such a menu. It was merely intended to squelch growling stomachs till the People could ride horse and buggy back home.

—from *The Betrayal*

(Note: See OLD-TIME LEMONADE on page 17.)

Therefore if thine enemy hunger, feed him; if he thirst, give him drink.

—ROMANS 12:20

SEAFOOD-FILLED MUSHROOMS

¹/₃ c. butter, melted

¹/₂ c. (rounded) plain un-seasoned bread crumbs

8 oz. imitation crabmeat, finely chopped

¹/₂ c. (rounded) very finely chopped onion

1 clove garlic, minced

¹/₃ c. butter, melted

32 medium mushrooms (approximately), stems removed

10 oz. Swiss cheese, grated

Heat ¹/₃ c. butter in cast-iron frying pan; sauté bread crumbs, crabmeat, onion, and garlic until lightly browned. Allow to cool until stuffing mixture can be handled easily.

Spray 9×13 glass baking dish with olive oil cooking spray; add ¹/₃ c. melted butter to cover bottom of baking dish. Place mushroom caps in baking dish and fill firmly with stuffing mixture. Fill in spaces in baking dish with any extra stuffing mixture. Top with Swiss cheese.

Bake at 400 degrees for 20–25 minutes; serve immediately. Leftovers are delicious, also! May be reheated.

Note: For two 10×15 glass baking dishes, triple this recipe.

Kissin' don't last; cookin' do!

REFRIED BEAN DIP

2 16-oz. cans refried beans
¼ tsp. garlic powder
½ large white onion, finely
  chopped
1 16-oz. jar chunky medium
  salsa

1 6-oz. can pitted black olives,
  sliced
2 16-oz. containers sour
  cream
12 oz. sharp white Cheddar
  cheese, grated

Mix refried beans, garlic powder, and chopped onion; spread in the bottom of a 9×13 glass baking dish. Spread salsa on top of bean mixture. Add layer of sliced black olives, reserving some for garnish. Spread sour cream on top of olives; top with grated cheese. Garnish with reserved olive slices.

Refrigerate. Serve with tortilla chips.

Note from Bev

A well-loved dip among the present-day Plain community in Lancaster County!

CHEESE BALLS

2 8-oz. packages cream
  cheese, softened
10 oz. extra-sharp white
  Cheddar cheese, grated
10 oz. extra-sharp Cheddar
  cheese, grated
8 oz. Monterey Jack cheese,
  grated
8 oz. Colby cheese, grated

8 oz. blue cheese, crumbled
4 tsp. Worcestershire sauce
½ tsp. lemon juice
¼ c. grated onion
2 tsp. dry mustard
½ tsp. salt
Pecans (optional)

Whip the cream cheese; add all other ingredients except pecans and mix well. Shape into three or four cheese balls. Top with finely chopped pecans if desired.

Note: These keep for several weeks in the refrigerator.

CREAMY GARDEN DELIGHT

8 oz. fresh mushrooms, sliced
1 large red bell pepper, cut
　into strips
2 small zucchini, sliced
1 large onion, sliced
2+ Tbsp. butter or olive oil
1½ tsp. salt, divided

42 saltine crackers (approximately)
1 lb. grated cheese—Pepper
　Jack or sharp Cheddar
¼ tsp. ground black pepper
5 eggs
1¾ c. milk

Sauté sliced mushrooms, pepper strips, zucchini, and onion slices in the butter or oil. Sprinkle with ½ tsp. salt.

Grease a 9×13 glass baking dish. Spread approximately 18 crackers in the bottom. Layer with half of the cooked vegetables, then half of the grated cheese. Sprinkle approximately ⅛ tsp. ground black pepper on top. Add another layer of approximately 24 crackers on top of cheese—then another layer of remaining vegetables, cheese, and black pepper. Beat eggs, milk, and remaining salt, and pour over mixture. Gently push vegetables, cheese, and crackers down into egg mixture until all is moistened. Bake at 350 degrees for approximately 40 minutes or until a sharp knife inserted in the center comes out clean.

LEMON JUBILEE PUNCH

1 6-oz. can frozen lemonade concentrate
1.5 6-oz. cans frozen orange juice concentrate (9 oz. total)
1 c. ginger ale, chilled

Prepare fruit juices as directed on cans and pour into punch bowl. Just before serving, add ice blocks and pour ginger ale slowly down inside of bowl. Makes 3 quarts.

East, west, home's best.

PEACHES-AND-CREAM MILK SHAKE

1 c. sliced peaches

1 pt. peach ice cream

1 c. milk, divided

Additional peach slices for garnish

Place peaches, ice cream, and ¼ cup milk in blender. Blend until softened. Add remaining milk and blend until mixed. Sweeten with a little sugar if desired. Pour into large glasses. Garnish each with fresh peach slice.

When April showers bring May flowers,
And tulips by the dozen,
A boy starts thinking of a girl,
One that's not his cousin.
—Author Unknown

PINEAPPLE-LIME FLOAT

1 12-oz. can pineapple juice

1 c. lime juice

⅔ c. sugar

Green food coloring

1 pt. lime sherbet

2 7-oz. bottles of ginger ale, chilled

Fresh mint (optional)

Combine pineapple juice, lime juice, sugar, and a few drops of food coloring; chill. Fill six glasses half full with juice mixture. Add a scoop of sherbet to each. Fill with ginger ale and garnish with fresh mint if desired.

HOT WASSAIL

1 gallon apple cider

1 cinnamon stick

½ tsp. nutmeg

1 tsp. whole cloves

1 can frozen orange juice concentrate

1 can frozen lemonade concentrate

Juice and rinds from 2 oranges and 1 lemon

Sugar to taste

Combine all ingredients and simmer for 3 hours. *Do not boil.*

Note from Bev

This lovely, warming drink was a welcome sight when Mother served it to my sister and me on blustery Pennsylvania nights. We especially enjoyed it at Christmastime and on New Year's Day.

Serve sun tea in mason jars for fun.

OLD-TIME LEMONADE

3 lemons
1/2 c. sugar

1 qt. water

Wash lemons. Squeeze juice from lemons into a large pitcher. Add sugar; fill pitcher with 1 qt. water. Chop rinds into 8–10 pieces and let soak in lemonade. Stir well until juice gets syrupy. Strain rinds out of juice and refrigerate.

Note from Bev

This homemade lemonade was always a big favorite at Buchwalter family picnics and all during the summer. Any time, really. The chopped lemon rinds make all the difference!

BIRD-IN-HAND EGGNOG

1 egg
2 Tbsp. sugar
Dash of salt

1 c. milk
1/2 tsp. vanilla
Nutmeg

Beat egg until thick. Stir in sugar and salt until sugar is dissolved. Mix milk and vanilla in with egg mixture, chill, and enjoy. Dust each serving with nutmeg for a spicy flavor.

PARTY PUNCH

1 46-oz. can pineapple juice,
chilled
3 c. cranberry juice, chilled

1 qt. ginger ale, chilled
1 lemon, thinly sliced

Combine all liquids in a large punch bowl. Float lemon slices on top.

Thou preparest a table before me in the presence of mine enemies . . . my cup runneth over. —PSALM 23:5

AUNT GLADYS'S CHOCOLATE MILK SHAKE

1½ c. whole milk
½ c. cold water
10 Tbsp. chocolate milk mix

2 oz. whipped topping
4 handfuls ice cubes
2 tsp. vanilla extract

Combine all ingredients in blender; blend until smooth. Serve cold.

Note from Bev

One of my aunt's mouth-watering recipes from the early 1930s.

FRUIT PUNCH

1 6-oz. can frozen orange
juice concentrate
2 6-oz. cans frozen limeade
concentrate
1 6-oz. can frozen lemonade
concentrate
1 can (1 lb., 14 oz.) pineapple
juice, chilled

2 c. cranberry juice, chilled
2–4 c. cold water
2 qts. ginger ale, chilled
1 qt. plain soda water, chilled
Fruit and mint for garnish

Empty all juices and water into large container; thaw and stir well. Pour mixture into punch bowl. Add ice cubes. Before serving, gently pour in ginger ale and soda water. Top with fruit ice ring (see recipe below) and sprigs of mint or fruit slices to garnish.

Makes 30 servings.

Note from Bev

I have served this delectable punch at various church and family gatherings, as well as at piano recitals throughout the years when I taught both voice and piano students. People always ask for the recipe. Enjoy!

FRUIT ICE RING

Use any combination of lime, lemon, or orange slices. Arrange in a pattern in bottom of 8-inch ring mold. Add water to cover the fruit; freeze. To remove ice ring from mold, dip bottom of mold into warm water. Float the ring on top of punch. Garnish with mint leaves and, if available, fresh strawberry slices.

IDA'S HOMEMADE TOMATO JUICE

1 peck (½ bushel) tomatoes or a 2-gallon crock full	3 stalks celery, chopped
	1 c. sugar
4 large peppers, chopped	2 Tbsp. salt
4 large onions, chopped	

Combine all ingredients in a large pot. Cook until soft, then strain. Bring to a rolling boil; bottle for canning.

Note: If unfamiliar with the canning process, a good resource is the *Ball Blue Book of Preserving* (available by calling 1-800-392-2575, option 1).

HOT COCOA

1 16-oz. can baking cocoa	8 oz. instant coffee creamer
32 c. powdered instant milk	1 lb. powdered sugar
(1 lb., 9.6 oz. box)	

Mix together all ingredients and store in a large container.
For a single serving, use 1–3 tsp. dry mix per cup of hot water.

Let not the sun go down upon your wrath.

–EPHESIANS 4:26

Breakfast Specialty Dishes

She headed downstairs to cook the usual breakfast for her dear ones. Abandoning thoughts of the past, she turned her attention to the future as she scrambled up nine large eggs, made cornmeal mush and fried potatoes, and set out plenty of toast, butter, grape jelly, and apple butter. Just knowing that she and Jacob and the children could move so far from home, that a Bible-based conservative group was expecting their arrival—or so Esther had said—filled her heart with gladness. The future was ever so bright.

—from *The Postcard*

(Note: See CORNMEAL MUSH on page 24.)

FRITTERS (APPLE OR ZUCCHINI)

Apple fritters:

2 c. dry pancake mix

$^1/_3$ c. oil

1 c. yogurt or sour milk

1 tsp. soda

Pinch of salt

$1^1/_2$ c. cut-up apples

Prepare batter by mixing together first five ingredients; stir in apples. Fry on lightly greased griddle. Serves 4.

Zucchini fritters:

Prepare batter as above, omitting apples and salt. Grind up 2 or 3 small zucchini, as well as $^1/_2$ c. grated Parmesan cheese; add to batter. Fry by dropping $^1/_2$ c. of batter on greased griddle. Serve hot and eat with syrup.

GRANDMA'S CORN FRITTERS

1 c. ground corn*

$1^1/_4$ c. milk

$^1/_2$ tsp. sugar

$^1/_2$ tsp. salt

1 tsp. baking powder

$^1/_2$ c. chopped cauliflower

1 egg

Combine corn and milk; let stand 30 minutes. Add remaining ingredients and fry until golden brown.

*Use ground corn or corn cut from the cob. It doesn't necessarily need to be ground; I've eaten corn fritters with whole, tender kernels of corn.

Note from Bev

It has been said no one could make a lighter, more delicate corn fritter than my own grandmother, Ada Buchwalter. She certainly had that innate "touch" every cook strives for in the kitchen.

CORNMEAL MUSH

6½ c. yellow cornmeal

½ c. flour

1 Tbsp. salt

4 c. cold water

2 c. cold milk

10 c. boiling water

olive oil

Mix cornmeal, flour, and salt together in a 6-qt. slow cooker. Gradually add cold water and milk; mix until smooth. Slowly add boiling water; stir in. Heat on high for approximately 2 hours, stirring with a wooden spoon every 10–15 minutes. Mixture will be thick and will not separate when done.

Fill 3 loaf pans with mixture; smooth tops. Cover each pan with plastic wrap, leaving two corners slightly open to let steam escape. Cool to room temperature; refrigerate overnight. (These will keep in refrigerator at least a week.)

Remove mixture from loaf pans; slice in pieces approximately ¼" thick.

Spray frying pan with olive oil cooking spray; add olive oil. Fry slices until nicely browned—approximately 5–8 minutes on first side, approximately 3–5 minutes on second side. Serve immediately with maple syrup or a thick corn syrup.*

*King's Syrup and Old Barrel table syrup are ideal for creating the true Pennsylvania Dutch taste. Other syrups are usually much too runny and will not create a satisfactory outcome.

I have esteemed the words of his mouth more than my necessary food.　　　　　　　　　　　　　　　　　　—JOB 23:12

BAKED EGGS

Cut out a round shape from a piece of toast and place in a muffin tin. Moisten slightly with milk. Break egg onto it and put in a slow oven (300 degrees) until desired consistency.

WAFFLES

2 c. flour	3 eggs, separated
2 tsp. baking powder	1½ c. milk
1 tsp. salt	3 Tbsp. shortening, melted
2 c. sugar	

Sift flour, baking powder, salt, and sugar together. Beat egg yolks well; gradually add yolks and milk to dry ingredients, mixing well. Add melted shortening. Beat egg whites until stiff; fold into batter. Bake on an evenly heated, well-greased waffle iron.

Note from Bev

This well-loved recipe came from my grandmother Ada's recipe file. Her wonderful waffles were served not only at breakfast but frequently at suppertime, as well, with tender pieces of cooked chicken and rich gravy.

BAKED OATMEAL

¼ c. cooking oil	1 tsp. cinnamon
½ c. sugar (white or brown)	1½ c. quick oats (or rolled
1 egg	oats)
1 tsp. baking powder	1 c. milk
½ tsp. salt	

Beat together all ingredients with mixing spoon; pour into greased 9×13 pan.

Bake at 275 degrees for 30 minutes or until done. Serve with milk.

Variations: Top baked oatmeal with ½ c. blueberries, raisins, diced bananas, or apples for a succulent option.

Easy Breakfast Soufflé

8 slices whole wheat bread, cut in cubes

1 lb. cheese, grated

1 1/2 c. chopped lean sausage, pre-cooked (lean ground beef can be used as a substitute)

6 eggs

3 c. whole milk

3/4 tsp. dry mustard

Salt and pepper

Layer bread cubes in a greased 9×13 pan, followed by a mixture of cheese, beaten eggs, milk, sausage, and seasonings to taste. Set overnight in refrigerator. Start in a cold oven; bake at 350 degrees for 45 minutes. Serve piping hot.

Note from Bev

What a way to begin the day! Your overnight guests will think you stayed up all night preparing this mouth-watering offering. I like to serve this with a variety of fresh seasonal fruit, along with apple juice and hot tea or coffee.

Do all the good you can,
By all the means you can,
In all the ways you can,
In all the places you can,
At all the times you can,
To all the people you can,
As long as ever you can.
—John Wesley's Rule

Honour thy father and thy mother: that thy days may be long upon the land which the Lord thy God giveth thee.

—EXODUS 20:12

BIRD'S NEST (OR EGG IN THE MIDDLE)

Bread slices (one per serving)   Honey
Eggs (one per slice of bread)   Cinnamon
Salt and pepper

Butter the sliced bread on one side. Place as many slices as desired on a greased cookie sheet, buttered side up. Using round cookie cutter, cut a hole in the middle of bread; set cutouts aside. Crack a raw egg into each cut-out circle; salt and pepper to taste.

Spread honey and cinnamon on the reserved cut-outs; place on the cookie sheet. Bake at 350 degrees for 10–15 minutes or until egg is firm.

Note from Bev

My mother often baked this tasty breakfast for my younger sister, Barbara, and me when we were growing up. She also served it on special days like Christmas morning or Thanksgiving Day. Mother created the recipe title, as well. Interestingly, it has stuck all these years.

Add diced or ground meat to omelets and soufflés.

CHOCOLATE WAFFLES

½ c. shortening

1 c. sugar

2 eggs, separated

2 1-oz. squares unsweetened chocolate

1½ c. cake flour (sifted before measuring)

2 tsp. baking powder

¼ tsp. salt

½ c. milk

¼ c. evaporated milk

¼ c. water

½ tsp. vanilla

Cream together shortening and sugar. Add well-beaten egg yolks; mix well. Melt chocolate in double boiler over hot water and add to creamed mixture; mix thoroughly.

Sift together the pre-sifted cake flour, baking powder, and salt. Mix milk, evaporated milk, and water together; add alternately with dry ingredients to chocolate mixture. Add flavoring; fold in stiffly beaten egg whites.

Serve with hot syrup, whipped cream, or ice cream. Makes 4 servings.

 Haste makes waste.

PERFECT PUMPKIN BREAD

3½ c. unsifted flour

3 c. sugar

2 tsp. baking soda

1½ tsp. salt

1 tsp. cinnamon

2 c. cooked fresh (or canned) pumpkin

1 c. vegetable oil

⅔ c. water

4 eggs

2 c. (12-oz. pkg.) peanut butter chips

1 c. chopped nuts

1 c. raisins (optional)

Grease and flour three loaf pans (8½×4½×2½ inches).

In medium mixing bowl, combine flour, sugar, baking soda, salt, and cinnamon; set aside. In large mixing bowl, blend pumpkin with oil, water, and eggs. Mix the dry ingredients in gradually until well blended. Stir in the peanut butter chips, nuts, and raisins.

Pour mixture into prepared pans and bake at 350 degrees for 50–60 minutes or until cake tester (or toothpick) comes out clean. Cool loaves in pans at least 10 minutes.

Serve with honey butter or whipped cream.

Note from Bev

Folks will ask for your recipe when you serve this. Also makes a nice light dessert at lunchtime or a midnight snack!

NO-BAKE GRANOLA BARS

Mix together the following ingredients:

5 c. oats	Nuts
4$^1/_2$ c. Rice Krispies cereal	Sunflower seeds
Raisins	Coconut

Mix the following in a separate bowl:

2 bags of small marshmal- lows*	$^1/_2$ c. peanut butter
	$^1/_4$ c. honey
1 c. butter	

Melt marshmallows and butter together; stir in peanut butter and honey. Add to dry ingredients; mix well. Press into greased 9×13 pan. Cut into squares and serve.

*Marshmallow crème may be substituted; mix in with melted butter.

She riseth also while it is yet night, and giveth meat to her household, and a portion to her maidens. —PROVERBS 31:15

Breads

Tomorrow, the Lord's Day, would be another story yet. There'd be no extra chores, just what had to be done in the barn—milkin' and whatnot. She would be cookin' food ahead for her siblings today. A right-gut baking ham was just the thing. She'd slice and serve it with other cold cuts tomorrow, along with strawberry-banana Jell-O, cup cheese, and homemade bread. Josiah had been beggin' for Apple Dapple cake here lately, so she'd prob'ly go ahead and bake some for the whole family.

—from *The Redemption of Sarah Cain*

(Note: See PRISCILLA'S HOMEMADE AMISH BREAD on page 35.)

WHOLE WHEAT ROLLS

1½ c. milk

½ c. sugar

2 tsp. salt

½ c. oil

2 Tbsp. dark molasses

2 c. whole wheat flour

2 ¼-oz. packages of yeast

1 c. warm water

4 eggs, beaten

7–7½ c. unbleached all-
    purpose flour

Mix together milk, sugar, salt, oil, molasses, and whole wheat flour; let soak overnight in the refrigerator.

In the morning, dissolve yeast in warm water. Remove milk and flour mixture from refrigerator; stir in dissolved yeast and beaten eggs. Mix in unbleached flour; knead. Let rise until approximately doubled in size, about one hour. Punch dough down and let rise again until doubled, about one hour. Roll dough out and cut with circle cookie cutter to desired size. Place on greased sheet. Let rise until approximately doubled in size. Bake at 350 degrees for 8–10 minutes.

Note: Makes a large quantity, but the rolls freeze very well.

MORNING GLORY MUFFINS

6 eggs

2½ c. sugar

2 c. oil

4 c. grated carrots

1 c. coconut

1 c. raisins

1 c. chopped nuts

2 c. grated apples

4 tsp. baking soda

1 tsp. salt

4 tsp. cinnamon

4 c. flour

Stir all ingredients together. Make as many muffins as desired, baking at 375 degrees for 20 minutes.

Note: This recipe makes quite a lot of batter. Extra batter will keep in refrigerator for up to 4 weeks.

Keep your eyes wide open before marriage, half shut afterwards.
—Benjamin Franklin

GREEN TOMATO BREAD

1 c. oil

3 eggs, beaten

2 c. sugar (or 1 c. honey)

1 tsp. vanilla

2 c. diced green tomatoes

3 c. flour

$\frac{1}{2}$ tsp. baking powder

$\frac{1}{4}$ tsp. baking soda

1 c. chopped nuts

1 c. raisins (optional)

Add oil to eggs, sugar or honey, vanilla, and tomatoes. Add dry ingredients to mixture and blend well. Stir in nuts and raisins. Pour into 2 greased loaf pans. Bake at 350 degrees for 40–45 minutes.

Man doth not live by bread only, but by every word that proceedeth out of the mouth of the Lord doth man live.

–DEUTERONOMY 8:3

PLAIN BISCUITS

1 c. sifted flour

2 tsp. baking powder

$\frac{1}{2}$ tsp. salt

3 Tbsp. margarine

$\frac{1}{3}$ c. milk

Preheat oven to 400 degrees. Sift together dry ingredients. Add margarine and milk; mix quickly. Knead on floured board and roll out $\frac{1}{2}$-inch thick; cut into rounds or squares. Bake on ungreased baking sheet for 20 minutes.

PRISCILLA'S HOMEMADE AMISH BREAD

2 $\frac{1}{4}$-oz. pkgs. active dry yeast

1 Tbsp. sugar

1 c. warm water

$\frac{1}{4}$ c. shortening

2 Tbsp. salt

$\frac{1}{2}$ c. sugar

1 c. boiling water

2$\frac{1}{2}$ c. warm water

10 c. (or more) flour

Dissolve yeast and 1 Tbsp. sugar in 1 c. warm water (not too hot). Set aside.

In a large mixing bowl, combine shortening, salt, sugar, and boiling water. Mix together until shortening is dissolved. Add 2$\frac{1}{2}$ c. of additional warm water. Now add the yeast mixture, and blend thoroughly in large bowl.

Next, add 5–6 cups of flour, gradually mixing until dough can no longer be mixed. Knead dough for 20 minutes, continuing to add the remaining flour until the dough becomes soft and is no longer sticky. Let rise for 2 hours.

Place dough in four bread pans, cover with a heavy cloth, and let rise for an additional two hours.

Bake at 350 degrees for 30 minutes.

Note from Bev

This bread is very appetizing!

Hospitality is making guests feel at home, even though you wish they were.
—Author unknown

PECAN ROLLS

Syrup:

2 Tbsp. butter

1/2 c. brown sugar

1/4 c. molasses

1 1/2 c. pecans

Rolls:

1 1/4-oz. pkg. yeast

1/4 c. warm water

1 c. scalded milk, cooled to
  lukewarm

1/4 c. sugar

1 tsp. salt

1 egg, beaten

3 1/2 c. flour, divided

1/4 c. margarine, melted

Butter and cinnamon

Syrup: Heat butter, sugar, and molasses until sugar is dissolved; stir in nuts. Pour syrup into two 9×13 pans; set aside.

Rolls: Dissolve yeast in warm water. Stir in milk, sugar, and salt. Add beaten egg, 1 3/4 c. flour, and melted margarine; mix well. Stir in remaining flour. Knead dough; let rise until double in size. Roll dough out to 3/4-inch thickness; spread with butter and cinnamon. Roll up and cut into 18 rolls. Place on top of syrup in prepared pans; let rise for 2 hours.

Bake rolls at 375 degrees for 25–30 minutes. Remove from oven; invert pans over a cookie sheet, allowing the remaining topping to drizzle over rolls.

Note from Bev

Pecan rolls bring back fondest memories of early Christmas morning and birthday time, as well. It's nearly impossible to eat only one! Also delicious served with hot tea or coffee!

*The hurrier I go,
the behinder I get.*

Banana Nut Bread

½ c. shortening	1 c. walnuts
1 c. sugar	2 c. flour
2 eggs, beaten	½ tsp. baking soda
1 c. mashed bananas	2 tsp. baking powder

Cream together shortening, sugar, eggs, bananas, and nuts. Add flour, soda, and baking powder; mix well. Bake in greased loaf pan at 350 degrees for 1 hour.

Variations:

(1) Substitute 1 c. applesauce for mashed bananas. Add ½ tsp. cinnamon and a dash of nutmeg or cloves. Optional: add raisins.
(2) Substitute 1 c. cooked rhubarb instead of mashed bananas.

Note from Bev

The light texture will convince banana bread connoisseurs on the very first bite!

Cinnamon Squares

2 8-oz. pkgs. crescent rolls	1 egg
2 8-oz. pkgs. cream cheese, softened	1 Tbsp. vanilla
1 c. sugar	¼ c. cinnamon-sugar

Unroll first package of crescent rolls; press into 9×13 pan. Mix together cream cheese, sugar, egg, and vanilla; spread over rolls. Unroll second package of rolls and arrange over top of mixture. Sprinkle with cinnamon-sugar. Bake at 350 degrees for 25 minutes.

The Lord is my light and my salvation; whom shall I fear? The Lord is the strength of my life; of whom shall I be afraid?
—PSALM 27:1

GRANDMA'S NUT LOAF

1 lb. dates

1 lb. English walnuts, shelled

1 c. flour, sifted

1 c. granulated sugar

2 tsp. baking powder

$\frac{1}{2}$ tsp. salt

4 eggs, separated

Mix together dates, walnuts, and dry ingredients. Beat egg yolks; stir in. Beat egg whites; fold into mixture. Bake in a greased loaf pan at 325–350 degrees for 1 hour.

HUSH PUPPIES

2 c. cornmeal

1 Tbsp. flour

$\frac{1}{2}$ tsp. baking soda

1 tsp. salt

1 egg, beaten

1 c. buttermilk

$\frac{1}{3}$ c. finely chopped onion

Oil

Mix together dry ingredients. Stir in egg, buttermilk, and onion. Pour oil $\frac{1}{2}$-inch deep in skillet and heat to 400 degrees. Drop batter by spoonfuls into oil and fry, turning occasionally. Drain on paper towels and serve piping hot. Recipe makes about 20 hush puppies, depending on size of spoonfuls.

PEANUT BUTTER BREAD

2 c. flour

4 tsp. baking powder

$\frac{1}{2}$ c. sugar

1 tsp. salt

$\frac{2}{3}$ c. peanut butter

1 c. milk

Sift together dry ingredients. Blend peanut butter and milk; add to dry ingredients. Pour batter into loaf pan that has been greased or lined with wax paper. Bake at 350 degrees for 45–50 minutes.

Use for sandwiches of cream cheese and tart jelly, such as grape or currant.

HONEY WHEAT RHUBARB MUFFINS OR CAKE

1/2 c. brown sugar, firmly packed

1/2 c. raw honey

1/2 c. oil

2 tsp. vanilla

1 c. buttermilk

1 1/2 c. diced rhubarb

1/2 c. chopped walnuts or pecans

1/3 c. bran (optional)

1/3 c. wheat germ

1/3 c. whole wheat flour

1 1/2 c. white flour

1 tsp. baking soda

1 tsp. baking powder

Topping:

1 Tbsp. butter, melted

2 Tbsp. honey

1 tsp. cinnamon

In a large bowl, mix together first five ingredients. Stir in rhubarb and nuts. In a second bowl, combine remaining ingredients. Fold slowly into the rhubarb mixture until well blended. Spoon batter into greased muffin tins, filling each cup two-thirds full. Mix together topping ingredients and sprinkle over each muffin. Bake at 400 degrees for 20–25 minutes. Makes 20 muffins.

Cake: Pour batter into greased loaf pans and bake at 400 degrees for 30–35 minutes or until done. Makes 2 cakes.

Judge not, and ye shall not be judged: condemn not, and ye shall not be condemned: forgive, and ye shall be forgiven: Give, and it shall be given unto you; good measure, pressed down, and shaken together, and running over. . . . For with the same measure that ye mete withal it shall be measured to you again.

—LUKE 6:37–38

AMISH FRIENDSHIP BREAD STARTER

Method 1: Covered glass or plastic container

1 c. flour   1 c. milk

1 c. sugar

Mix all ingredients together in a glass or plastic container and follow the steps below. Do not refrigerate. Keep securely covered at room temperature from Day 1 through Day 10.

* Day 1: Make or receive starter.
* Day 2: Stir and cover—do not use a metal utensil to stir.
* Day 3: Stir.
* Day 4: Stir.
* Day 5: Add 1 c. each of flour, sugar, and milk.
* Day 6: Stir.
* Day 7: Stir.
* Day 8: Let stand—do not stir.
* Day 9: Let stand—do not stir.
* Day 10: Make Friendship Bread (see following recipe); do not stir or disturb until making bread.

Method 2: Ziplock freezer bag

$1/2$ c. flour (regular or $1/2$ c. milk (store-bought or
    unbleached)   raw goat's milk)

$1/2$ c. sugar (white granulated
    or raw)

Mix all ingredients together and put in a 1-gallon ziplock freezer bag, making sure the zipper is clean and seals well. Follow the steps below. Do not refrigerate; let sit at room temperature in a place where it can rise.

* Day 1: Make starter and put in sealed bag.
* Day 2: Squish bag to mix thoroughly.*
* Day 3: Squish bag to mix thoroughly.
* Day 4: Squish bag to mix thoroughly.
* Day 5: Squish bag to mix thoroughly.

* Day 6: Add 2 c. flour, 1 c. sugar, and 1 c. milk. Squish bag to mix thoroughly.
* Day 7: Squish bag and let air out—be careful that the zipper is clean before resealing. (Note: you may have to let air out before squishing bag.)
* Day 8: Squish bag and let air out—be careful that the zipper is clean before resealing. (Note: you may have to let air out before squishing bag.)
* Day 9: Squish bag and let air out—be careful that the zipper is clean before resealing. (Note: you may have to let air out before squishing bag.)
* Day 10: Make Friendship Bread (see following recipe); do not squish or disturb bag until making bread.

Starter can be used to make approximately 4 cups of new starter. On Day 10, you can make four batches of Friendship Bread or make one batch of bread and give three 1-cup starters to friends. Alternatively, you can make three batches of Friendship Bread and save 1 cup starter for yourself.

*Starting with Day 2, it may be necessary to let excess air out of the bag one or more times per day; be careful not to disturb starter while doing so.

FRIENDSHIP BREAD

Cinnamon

Sugar

1 c. oil

3 large eggs

1/2 c. milk

1 tsp. vanilla

2 c. flour

1 c. sugar

1 1/2 tsp. baking powder

1/2 tsp. salt

1/2 tsp. baking soda

2 tsp. cinnamon

1 large box of instant vanilla pudding (or 3/4 c. [rounded] bulk instant vanilla pudding)

1 c. baking raisins (or soak raisins 5 minutes in hot water, then drain well)

1 c. flour

1 c. sugar

1 c. milk

Preheat oven to 325 degrees. In a small bowl, make a mixture of sugar and cinnamon. Prepare two loaf pans, one Bundt pan, or a 9×13 baking dish by greasing the pans and coating with the cinnamon-sugar mixture, reserving some for topping. (Note: Tin loaf pans are excellent for making Friendship Bread.) Set aside.

Combine oil, eggs, ½ c. milk, and vanilla in a large glass or non-metal bowl, mixing well. Add 2 c. flour, 1 c. sugar, baking powder, salt, baking soda, cinnamon, pudding, and raisins to egg mixture; do not mix.

In separate medium glass or nonmetal bowl, using wooden spoon, mix together 1 c. flour and 1 c. sugar. Gradually add 1 c. milk, keeping mixture smooth. Add Amish Friendship Bread Starter from container or plastic bag, mixing in gently with a wooden spoon. Add approximately 1 cup of the resulting mixture into the egg/flour/raisin mixture. With a wooden spoon, mix egg/flour/raisin/starter mixture together well.

Pour batter into the prepared pans; sprinkle reserved cinnamon-sugar mixture on top. Bake at 325 degrees for approximately 1 hour or until toothpick inserted in center comes out clean. Do not over-bake. Allow to cool in pans. This bread freezes well.

Of the remaining new starter mixture, put 1 c. each into three plastic or glass containers or gallon ziplock freezer bags. Keep one starter for yourself and give two starters to friends with the instructions for Amish Friendship Bread Starter (today is Day 1), or make additional batches of Friendship Bread to give away.

One batch Friendship Bread makes two loaf pans, one Bundt pan, or one 9×13 cake pan.

Variations: Add chopped nuts, dates, or chocolate chips to the batter before baking. For a different flavor, a pudding mix other than vanilla may be used.

Note from Bev

The original idea of this unique recipe was to share either starter or baked bread with friends or family. A thoughtful gift!

DATE AND NUT BREAD

1 c. boiling water	$3/4$ c. sugar
$1^{1}/_2$ c. pitted dates, cut fine	1 tsp. vanilla
with scissors	$1/_2$ tsp. salt (scant)
1 tsp. soda	2 c. sifted flour
1 egg	$3/4$ c. chopped nuts

Pour boiling water over dates. Add soda and let mixture cool. In separate bowl, beat egg; add sugar and mix well. Stir in date mixture and remaining ingredients; mix well. Bake in loaf pan, greased or lined with wax paper, for 1 hour or more at 350 degrees. Ice with plain frosting if desired.

Note from Bev

Very nice sliced thin and served with Velveeta cheese.

BARBIE'S ZUCCHINI BREAD

3 eggs	1 tsp. cinnamon
$1^{3}/_4$ c. sugar (or $1/_2$ c. honey)	1 tsp. baking soda
1 c. oil	1 tsp. baking powder
2 c. grated zucchini	3 c. flour
1 tsp. vanilla	

Combine first five ingredients until smooth. Add cinnamon, baking soda, and baking powder. Gradually add flour and mix until thoroughly combined. Pour batter into 2 large, greased loaf pans. Bake at 375 degrees for 55 minutes.

Note from Bev

Barbara, my sister, passed this recipe along to me years ago. My granddaughter, Ariel, likes to put jelly or honey on top . . . sometimes whipped cream. I know you'll love it, too!

Whither thou goest, I will go; and where thou lodgest, I will lodge: thy people shall be my people, and thy God my God.

—RUTH 1:16

IRENE'S HOMEMADE BREAD

5 c. whole wheat flour	2 eggs, beaten
1 c. sugar	²⁄₃ c. oil
1 Tbsp. salt	5 c. very warm water
¼ c. yeast	9 c. high-gluten white flour or bread flour

Combine 3 cups whole wheat flour, sugar, salt, and yeast and mix with wooden spoon. Add eggs, oil, and water; mix well. Add remaining whole wheat flour and mix in. Add high-gluten or bread flour, 3 cups at a time, till approximately 8 cups are stirred in. Save the ninth cup to add while kneading dough.

Dump dough on floured board and knead about 10 minutes, adding reserved flour as needed until dough is a smooth consistency. Put a little oil in mixing bowl and put dough back in, oiling both sides lightly. Let rise 20 minutes. Punch down and let rise approximately 1 hour. Punch down; shape into 6 (1½ pounds each) loaves. Place in greased bread pans and let rise about 1 hour or until dough rises above pans. Bake at 300 degrees for 25 to 30 minutes. Cool on wire rack about 30 minutes or until cool enough to bag.

Note from Bev

The Mennonites first developed the type of wheat for high-gluten white flour in Russia and brought it with them when they migrated to "Penn's Woods"—Pennsylvania—in the early 1700s.

Salads and Salad Dressings

Ida went about her kitchen work, sweeping and washing the floor. She began cooking the noon meal for Abram and the girls, knowing how awful hungry her husband, and Leah, too, would be when they came in from the barn around eleven-thirty or so, eager for a nice meal. Today it was meatball chowder, homemade bread and butter, cottage cheese salad, and chocolate revel bars, Abram's favorite dessert.

—from *The Covenant*

(Note: See COTTAGE CHEESE AND PEPPER SALAD on page 55.)

GRANDMA BUCHWALTER'S TUNA SALAD

6 hard-boiled eggs, mashed
Mayonnaise
1 6-oz. can tuna

¹/₂ c. diced celery
Lettuce
Paprika

Mix eggs and desired amount of mayonnaise together; stir in tuna and celery. Using an ice cream dipper, make balls of tuna mixture and place on lettuce "cups." Sprinkle with paprika.

Note from Bev

This is my grandmother's exquisite recipe. The amount of eggs makes the tuna salad delicate and light as a feather!

WALDORF SALAD

1 celery stem, chopped
1 apple, diced
2 Tbsp. mayonnaise

1 Tbsp. raisins
Lettuce

Stir celery, apple, mayonnaise, and raisins together; dish onto washed and dried lettuce cups. Add your choice of garnish.

PERFECTION SALAD

1 c. boiling water
1 3-oz. package lemon-
    flavored gelatin
2 Tbsp. lemon juice or vinegar
1 tsp. salt
1 c. cold water

1 c. finely diced celery
1 c. finely shredded cabbage
2 Tbsp. finely chopped
    pimiento
¹/₃ c. chopped sweet pickles

Pour boiling water over gelatin in bowl, stirring until dissolved. Stir in lemon juice, salt, and cold water. Chill until slightly thickened but not set. Stir in celery, cabbage, pimiento, and pickles. Pour into 6 to 8 individual molds; chill until firm.

CHICKEN SALAD

2 c. diced cooked chicken	1/4 tsp. onion powder
1 1/2 c. sliced celery	1/4 tsp. pepper
3/4 tsp. salt	1/3 c. mayonnaise
1/2 tsp. powdered mustard	2 tsp. lemon juice

In a large bowl, combine chicken, celery, salt, mustard, onion powder, and pepper. Stir in mayonnaise and lemon juice. Cover and refrigerate until chilled and ready to serve.

To frost grapes: Dip tiny bunches of washed grapes into lemon juice. Then sprinkle with granulated sugar. Dry on wire rack. A tasty garnish for that special fruit salad or other dishes.

CRANBERRY GRAPE SALAD

1 lb. cranberries, fresh or frozen	1 c. chopped nut meats
1 2/3 c. sugar	12 large marshmallows, quartered
2 c. Tokay grapes or other red grapes, halved and seeded	1 c. whipped cream
1 c. sliced celery	Lettuce

Grind cranberries through fine blade of food chopper into a medium bowl; drain. Add sugar to ground cranberries; set aside. Combine all other ingredients except lettuce and fold together thoroughly; fold in cranberries. Chill for several hours. Serve in lettuce cups.

And the fruit of righteousness is sown in peace of them that make peace.

—JAMES 3:18

GINGER ALE SALAD

Salad:

1 20-oz. can crushed
  pineapple
2 Tbsp. unflavored gelatin
2 Tbsp. water
³/₄ c. sugar

1 c. hot water
Juice of 1 lemon
1 pt. ginger ale
1 c. seedless red grapes,
  halved

Dressing:

2 Tbsp. flour
¹/₂ c. sugar
2 eggs, beaten
1¹/₂ Tbsp. butter, melted

Pineapple juice (reserved from
  canned pineapple, above)
1 c. whipped cream

Salad: Drain pineapple, reserving juice; set aside. Dissolve gelatin in 2 Tbsp. water; stir well. Add sugar and hot water to gelatin, mixing well. Stir in lemon juice and ginger ale; refrigerate until almost firm. Fold in pineapple and grapes. Chill. Serve topped with dressing.

Dressing: Mix flour and sugar well. Add eggs, butter, and reserved juice; cook until thick. Let cool. Fold in whipped cream.

LIME PINEAPPLE CHEESE

1 8-oz. can crushed pineapple,
  undrained
1 3-oz. box lime Jell-O

1 lb. cottage cheese
1 c. heavy cream, whipped

Heat crushed pineapple to a boil. Dissolve Jell-O in hot pineapple. Cool. Fold in cottage cheese and whipped cream. Pour in salad bowl; chill.

MOLDED CUCUMBER SALAD

1½ Tbsp. gelatin
1 c. boiling water
½ c. cold water
2 c. heavy cream, whipped
2 cucumbers, washed
1 tsp. salt

1 sweet pimiento, chopped
1 tsp. lemon juice
½ green pepper, chopped
Lettuce
Pimiento
Parsley

Dissolve gelatin in boiling water; add to cold water and let sit for 5 minutes. Fold the whipped cream into the gelatin.

Pare and dice the cucumbers; mix together with salt, pimiento, lemon juice, and green pepper. Fold into gelatin mixture. Pour into a chilled wet mold. When set, serve on lettuce, garnished with pimiento and some parsley.

Waste not; want not.

BROCCOLI AND CAULIFLOWER SALAD

2 c. mayonnaise
1 c. sugar
½ tsp. salt
¼ c. vinegar
2 Tbsp. mustard

1 medium head broccoli, florets only
1 medium head cauliflower, florets only

Mix all ingredients except vegetables together until smooth. Chop broccoli and cauliflower very fine; toss with dressing.

Note from Bev

This dressing is also good for potato or macaroni salads or coleslaw. For a cucumber and onion salad, add a little sour cream to the dressing, mix with chopped cucumbers and onions, and garnish with raisins.

SALMON AND EGG SALAD

1 8-oz. can salmon (or tuna if
   preferred)
3 hard-boiled eggs, chopped

1 stalk celery, chopped
2 Tbsp. mayonnaise
Lettuce (optional)

Mix all ingredients together lightly with fork. Serve on lettuce, or spread on toast for sandwich.

In quietness and confidence shall be your strength.

—ISAIAH 30:15

SUNSHINE SALAD

1 3-oz. box orange Jell-O
1/4 tsp. salt
1 c. boiling water
1 c. cold water

Juice of 2 lemons
1/2 c. crushed pineapple
3/4 c. grated carrots

Stir all ingredients together. Chill until firm; serve.

MISTY MINT SALAD

1 20-oz. can crushed
   pineapple
1 pkg. unflavored gelatin

1/2 c. mint-flavored apple jelly
2 c. whipped cream
Grated carrots (optional)

Drain pineapple, reserving juice. Set aside. Use the juice to soften gelatin. After gelatin is softened, place in a saucepan over low heat, stirring constantly until dissolved. Add jelly and stir until melted. Remove from heat; add pineapple. If desired, grated carrots may be added for color. Chill until thick and syrupy. Fold in whipped cream; turn into a lightly oiled 4-cup mold. Chill until set.

Simple Salads

Arrange the following salads on a salad plate:

Salad #1:

1 large lettuce leaf (cup shape)

1 sliced tomato

1/2 hard-boiled egg, sliced

Grated cheese on top

Add a dab of homemade mayonnaise.

Salad #2:

1 large lettuce leaf (cup shape)

1 slice pineapple

2 slices peach or apricot

Top with dab of whipped cream.

Salad #3:

1 large lettuce leaf (cup shape)

1 dip of potato salad (use ice cream dipper to shape)

Top with a green olive.

Salad #4:

1 large lettuce leaf (cup shape)

1 slice pineapple

1/2 banana (slices arranged on edge of pineapple)

Whipped cream or homemade mayonnaise

Top with a cherry.

Homemade Mayonnaise Dressing

1 Tbsp. flour

3 Tbsp. sugar

2 eggs

Big pinch of salt (less than 1/2 tsp.)

1/2 c. vinegar (scant)

Butter

Mix together flour and sugar. Beat eggs thoroughly; add to flour and sugar. Mix in salt and vinegar.

Melt butter the size of an egg in saucepan. Pour egg mixture in and let cook until thick, stirring constantly. When mixture has thickened, remove pan from heat, pour mixture into bowl, and beat with egg beater until light and smooth. Refrigerate.

The fruit of the Spirit is love, joy, peace, longsuffering, gentle-ness, goodness, faith, meekness, temperance.

—GALATIANS 5:22–23

MIXED VEGETABLE SALAD

Grind young, raw carrots, turnips, cabbage, sweet pepper, onion, and radishes through a food processor, using the finest setting. Mix with mayonnaise and serve on lettuce.

RAW BEET AND CARROT SALAD

1 c. grated young carrot

½ c. grated young beet

⅓ c. mayonnaise

Mix and serve on lettuce.

SPINACH AND CARROT SALAD

½ c. finely chopped raw spinach

1 c. grated raw carrot

⅓ c. mayonnaise

Mix and serve on lettuce.

CABBAGE, PEPPER, AND CARROT SALAD

½ c. ground cabbage

¾ c. ground carrot

½ c. ground sweet pepper

⅓ c. mayonnaise

Mix and serve on lettuce.

EGG, CABBAGE, AND SWEET PEPPER SALAD

1 c. chopped cabbage

2 hard-boiled eggs, chopped

1 Tbsp. chopped pepper

⅓ c. mayonnaise

Mix and serve on lettuce.

'Tis the gift to be simple,
'Tis the gift to be free,
'Tis the gift to come down
Where we ought to be.
—Shaker Hymn, 1848

STUFFED TOMATOES WITH COTTAGE CHEESE

Scald and peel firm tomatoes. Lay each one on a plate, stem end down. Cut two slits from top down toward the stem end in such a way as to remove a wedge-shaped piece. Then cut out similar wedged-shaped pieces from the sides of the tomato midway between the bottom and the opening made in the top. Fill openings with cottage cheese. Place on lettuce and surround with plenty of mayonnaise.

PEACH SALAD

Peel large ripe peaches. Halve; remove pits. Place on lettuce and fill peach cavities with red raspberries. Serve with whipped cream.

PINEAPPLE FRUIT SALAD

4 slices pineapple	4 thin orange slices
4 lettuce leaves	4 red cherries
1/3 c. mayonnaise	

Place pineapple on lettuce leaves and spread with mayonnaise. Add orange slices and top with cherries. Makes 4 servings.

Add garden mint to fruit salads or a
sprig atop a bowl of blueberries.

COTTAGE CHEESE AND PEPPER SALAD

2 c. cottage cheese

½ c. sour cream

1 small onion, diced

1 green pepper, diced

Salt and pepper

Crisp lettuce "cups"

1 Tbsp. chopped watercress or parsley

Blend cottage cheese and sour cream with a fork. Add vegetables and mix well. Season to taste. Serve cold on crisp lettuce "cups." Garnish with watercress or parsley.

PAPPA'S POTATO SALAD

3 lbs. potatoes

3 stalks celery

½ onion

2 Tbsp. sugar

2 Tbsp. vinegar

1 tsp. salt

⅛ tsp. pepper

1 c. mayonnaise

1 c. sour cream

Cook potatoes in salted water until tender; drain and cool. Peel potatoes and cut into small squares. Cut celery and onion into very small pieces and add to potatoes; set aside.

In saucepan, mix together sugar, vinegar, salt, and pepper. Cook, stirring, until sugar dissolves; remove from heat. Cool. Stir in mayonnaise and sour cream.

Toss sour cream mixture with potatoes, celery, and onion. If salad is too dry, cream may be added. Refrigerate until ready to serve.

Let your moderation be known unto all men.

–PHILIPPIANS 4:5

INDIANA AMISH SALAD

Salad:

2 6-oz. pkgs. lemon Jell-O

4 c. boiling water

1 20-oz. can crushed
  pineapple

2 c. whipping cream

1 8-oz. package cream cheese

Topping:

3 egg yolks, lightly beaten

1 c. granulated sugar

Pineapple juice (reserved from
  salad) plus water to equal
  $3^{1/2}$ cups

2 rounded Tbsp. cornstarch

1 c. water

Salad: Dissolve Jell-O in boiling water; refrigerate until partially set. Meanwhile, drain pineapple, reserving juice. Stir pineapple into slightly set Jell-O. Beat whipping cream and cream cheese together in a large mixing bowl until light. Gradually fold Jell-O into cream cheese mixture. Pour into a 9×13 pan; cover and chill.

Topping: Beat egg yolks and sugar together in a large saucepan. (Be careful not to let mixture boil over.) Combine reserved pineapple juice with water to make $3^{1/2}$ cups of liquid; gradually stir into the sugar and egg yolks, keeping mixture smooth. In a separate small bowl, slowly stir in 1 c. water to cornstarch, stirring until smooth. And water and cornstarch to mixture in saucepan and bring to a boil; reduce heat. Simmer over medium heat until thick, about 30 minutes, stirring frequently. Cool to room temperature and spread evenly on chilled salad. (Topping will thicken.) Keep refrigerated until ready to serve.

Too soon old, too late smart.

AVOCADO AND EGG SALAD

4 hard-boiled eggs, chopped

4 slices crisp bacon, crumbled

1 Tbsp. finely chopped green onion

2 large avocados, halved and pitted

2 Tbsp. mayonnaise

2 tsp. lemon juice

1 tsp. prepared mustard

1/4 tsp. salt

Dash of pepper

Lettuce

Bacon for garnish

Combine eggs, bacon, and onion. Carefully scoop out avocado halves, leaving shells firm, and brush insides of shells with a little lemon juice. Mash avocado and stir in remaining ingredients. Add egg mixture and spoon into avocado shells. Serve each shell on lettuce with a bacon curl.

Note from Bev

Mm-m! Lunchtime doesn't get better than this. Nice and light!

STUFFED TOMATO SALAD

4 medium tomatoes (1 per serving)

2 hard-boiled eggs (one half per serving)

1/4 c. diced cucumber

1 stalk celery, chopped

Chopped radish

Mayonnaise to taste

Fresh parsley

Lettuce

Carve out top of tomato with a sharp knife. Scoop out the contents and set aside. Halve eggs; remove and mash egg yolks. Chop egg whites. Mix diced cucumber, chopped celery, chopped egg white, and radish with the tomato contents, adding mayonnaise to moisten. Fill each tomato with the mixture and sprinkle egg yolk on top. Add spray of parsley and serve on lettuce.

MANDARIN ORANGE SALAD

Salad:

1/4 c. slivered almonds

4 tsp. sugar

1/4 head iceberg lettuce

1/4 head romaine lettuce

2 stalks celery, sliced

2 onions, thinly sliced

1 11-oz. can mandarin
oranges, drained

Dressing:

1/4 c. canola oil

2 Tbsp. sugar

2 Tbsp. vinegar

1 Tbsp. chopped parsley

1/2 tsp. salt

Dash pepper

Salad: Cook almonds and sugar over low heat until sugar is melted. Cool.

Tear lettuce into bite-size pieces. Add celery, onion, oranges, and almonds. Top with dressing just before serving.

Dressing: Mix all ingredients together thoroughly and serve over salad.

PINEAPPLE SHERBET SALAD

1 3-oz. box orange Jell-O

1 c. hot water

1 pt. pineapple sherbet

1 8-oz. can mandarin oranges,
drained

1 banana, sliced

1 20-oz. can crushed pineapple, drained

Combine all ingredients. Chill and serve.

Note from Bev

One of my mother's favorites . . . mine, too!

APPLESAUCE SALAD

2 c. sweetened applesauce
1 3-oz. box lime Jell-O
1 7-oz. bottle 7-Up

1 c. chopped celery
1/2 c. chopped nuts

Heat applesauce until hot enough to dissolve gelatin. Remove from heat and stir in Jell-O. Allow to cool but not thicken. Add 7-Up, celery, and nuts. Mix well, pour into molds, and chill.

HICKORY HOLLOW SALAD

1 large pineapple
1 c. shredded lettuce
4 oz. cooked ham (cut into strips)

4 oz. cooked turkey (cut into strips)
4 oz. sharp cheese (cut into strips)

Cut pineapple in half lengthwise. Remove hard center core. Using a small knife, cut around edge of fruit, leaving 1/2-inch rim. Remove and dice loosened fruit. Arrange in pineapple shells with lettuce, ham, and turkey strips. Top with cheese strips.

LETTUCE SALAD

Salad:

1 head of lettuce, rinsed, drained, and torn up
1/2 large white onion, chopped

4 hard-boiled eggs, sliced
10 oz. Swiss cheese, grated

Dressing:

1 c. Miracle Whip Light
1/2 c. sugar

1 Tbsp. apple cider vinegar
3–4 Tbsp. milk

Mix dressing ingredients together; set aside. Starting with lettuce, layer all salad ingredients. Pour dressing over the top; toss together. (Lettuce will wilt.) May also serve the salad layered and add salad dressing to taste.

Look before you leap.
—English Proverb

Dawdi Fisher's Potato Salad

Salad:

5 lbs. potatoes, unpeeled

2 stalks celery

1 large white onion

5 hard-boiled eggs

Sauce:

2 c. Miracle Whip Light

2/3 c. sugar

1/4 c. stone-ground mustard

2 Tbsp. (or less) apple cider
   vinegar

2–3 tsp. salt

Salad: Cook potatoes in salted water until firm-soft; peel and cut into small pieces. Cut celery, onion, and eggs into very small pieces and add to potatoes; mix together lightly. Add sauce; mix lightly. Refrigerate.

Sauce: Mix together Miracle Whip and sugar. Add mustard, vinegar, and salt; blend well. Keep refrigerated.

Variation: Spaghetti Salad

Boil 1 lb. angel hair spaghetti according to directions on package, breaking pasta in half before putting into boiling water. Run cold water over cooked spaghetti until cool. Drain well and use in place of potatoes.

Cucumber Salad

1 cucumber, peeled and sliced
   fine

1 onion, sliced fine

1/2 c. Miracle Whip Light

1/4 c. sugar

1/2 tsp. vinegar

Combine cucumbers and onion in bowl. Mix together remaining ingredients and add to vegetables. Chill.

BLUE CHEESE DRESSING

1 c. mayonnaise

$1/2$ c. crumbled blue cheese

$1/2$ c. sour cream

$1/3$ c. milk

1 Tbsp. sugar

2 Tbsp. white vinegar

1 tsp. Worcestershire sauce

$1/2$ tsp. salt

$1/8$ tsp. black pepper

1 garlic clove, minced

Stir together all ingredients in medium bowl; cover and chill. Serve over tossed greens or mixed vegetables. (Stir in additional milk if dressing thickens upon standing.)

A fat wife and a big barn never did a man any harm.

OLD-FASHIONED SOUR CREAM DRESSING

$1/2$ c. sour cream

2 Tbsp. vinegar

$1/2$ tsp. salt

2 Tbsp. sugar

Paprika

Beat all ingredients together until mixture is stiff. Serve with shredded cabbage or as a dressing for salads.

Soups and Stews

And my, oh my, Sadie could clean and cook like a house a-fire. Nobody around these parts, or in all of Lancaster County for that matter, could redd up a place faster or make a tastier beef stew. But those were just two of Sadie's many talents.

—from *The Covenant*

(Note: see SADIE'S BEEF STEW on page 65.)

SADIE'S BEEF STEW

3 lb. beef (round or rump)

Salt and pepper to taste

1/4 tsp. crumbled saffron
threads

2 Tbsp. gelatin

2 carrots, diced

3 Tbsp. uncooked rice

2 Tbsp. barley

1 c. pinto beans (boiled soft)

2 stalks blanched celery,
chopped

1 head of cabbage, chopped

1 onion, chopped

1 ear of corn (kernels only)

1 1/2 Tbsp. alphabet pasta

2 potatoes, peeled and diced

Cut beef into stew-size pieces; add enough water to cover by an inch. Boil beef for 2 hours. Add salt, pepper, saffron, and gelatin; boil for an additional hour. Stir in all remaining ingredients except for potatoes; boil for 15 minutes. Add potatoes and boil for an additional 30 minutes or until vegetables are tender.

Her children arise up, and call her blessed; her husband also, and he praiseth her.   —PROVERBS 31:28

SATURDAY SOUP

2 lbs. soup bones or stewing
meat

Salt and pepper

4–5 large potatoes, diced

1 c. diced carrots

1 c. diced onion

1 1/2 c. green beans (frozen or
canned)

Dash curry powder

2 bay leaves

In kettle, cover soup bones or stewing meat with water; add salt and pepper to taste. Simmer for at least 1 hour; remove soup bones from liquid. Add remaining ingredients; mix together with broth. Simmer for several hours.

Corn Chowder

6 medium potatoes
1/2 lb. bacon
2 small onions, diced
4 c. milk
1 tsp. salt

1 1/2 c. corn
1/2 tsp. pepper
2 tsp. parsley flakes
Potato flakes (optional)

Cut potatoes into bite-size pieces, boil until soft, drain. Dice bacon and fry until almost crisp; drain. Add onions to bacon; cook until tender. Heat milk, but do not boil. Add bacon and onions to warming milk; stir in potatoes and remaining ingredients. Add potato flakes to thicken if desired. Let simmer for 1 hour.

Let us therefore follow after the things which make for peace, and things wherewith one may edify another.

—ROMANS 14:19

Hearty Vegetable Soup

6–8 potatoes, peeled and chopped
1 1/2 c. diced carrots
1 1/2 c. sweet peas
2 10.75-oz. cans tomato soup
1 10.75-oz. can cream of mushroom soup
1 c. brown rice

1 Tbsp. oregano
1/2 tsp. chili powder
1 tsp. celery seed
1 tsp. tarragon
1/2 tsp. garlic powder
1 beef bouillon cube
1/2 c. cornstarch
8 c. hot water

In a large kettle, combine all ingredients. Bring to a boil for 10 minutes. Simmer for 1 hour or until vegetables are soft. Salt and pepper to taste. Enjoy!

*Save meat bones for making soup
stock with vegetables.*

WISE WOMAN'S SOUP

5–6 large potatoes, peeled and diced

1 10.75-oz. can cream of mushroom soup

1 10-oz. can chicken broth

3 bay leaves

1 10.75-oz. can chicken and rice soup

1 Tbsp. oregano

1 tsp. parsley flakes

1 tsp. celery seed

3/4 c. whole milk

2 cups corn (frozen or canned)

1 c. green beans

1/2 c. diced carrots

1/2 c. diced celery

1 medium onion, diced

Salt and pepper

Fill a large kettle two-thirds full of water, add potatoes, and bring to a rolling boil. Add remaining ingredients. Let boil 10 minutes more. Simmer 2–3 hours. Salt and pepper to taste.

KATIE FISHER'S BEEF STEW

2 Tbsp. butter

2 lbs. beef (cubed)

1 large onion

1 clove garlic

4 c. boiling water

1 Tbsp. salt

1 Tbsp. lemon juice

1 tsp. sugar

1 tsp. Worcestershire sauce

1/2 tsp. pepper

1/2 tsp. paprika

1 or 2 bay leaves

Dash of cloves or allspice

6 carrots, chopped

1 lb. small onions

6 med. potatoes, peeled and diced

1/2 c. cold water

1/4 c. flour

Brown meat in butter. Add next 11 ingredients and simmer for 2 hours. Add carrots, onions, potatoes, and paste made of water and flour; cook an additional 30 minutes.

CREAMY POTATO SOUP

10 potatoes, diced

2 c. water

1 c. chopped onions (or more)

1 tsp. salt

1 stalk celery, finely chopped

2 c. whole milk

Butter

3–4 hard-boiled eggs

Parsley (optional)

Combine potatoes, water, onion, salt, and celery in large saucepan; bring to a boil. Do not drain. When potatoes are soft, add milk and a large pat of butter; heat through. Season with salt and pepper. Meanwhile, peel the hard-boiled eggs, chopping the egg whites and fork-mashing the yolks.

To serve, sprinkle each serving with a couple of tablespoons of finely mashed egg yolk. Add the chopped whites to the individual servings, as well. Sprinkle with parsley if desired.

Note: The hard-boiled eggs help to round out the meal, along with either toasted or buttered whole grain bread.

ASPARAGUS SOUP

2 c. asparagus

$1/4$ c. butter

$1/4$ c. flour

$1/4$–$1/2$ tsp. salt

2 c. milk

8 oz. sharp white Cheddar
cheese, shredded

Cut asparagus into 1" pieces (cut with a sharp knife from the top down to where stalk gets tough). Cover with salted water and cook until tender; do not overcook. Do not drain.

Melt butter in saucepan; mix in flour and salt. Simmer mixture while gradually adding milk, stirring constantly. Boil mixture until smooth and fairly thick. If necessary, add a bit of extra milk to keep smooth. Add cheese. After cheese is melted, mix some of the liquid from the asparagus into the cheese mixture to thin it down. Add cheese sauce to asparagus and water; mix until well combined. Heat soup through but do not boil. Serve immediately.

Meatball Stew

1 lb. lean ground beef
1/4 c. fine dry bread crumbs
1/4 c. chopped onion
1 egg
1 tsp. salt
2 Tbsp. oil
2 c. tomato sauce

1 c. thinly sliced carrots
1 Tbsp. sugar
1/8 tsp. basil leaves (or parsley flakes)
1 lb. small potatoes (approximately 4), cut up
2 Tbsp. flour

Mix the first 5 ingredients well and shape into 16 meatballs. Brown in oil in skillet; pour off the fat. Add 1½ c. tomato sauce along with the next 3 ingredients. Cover and cook over low heat for 15 minutes, stirring occasionally. Add potatoes and cook 5 minutes longer or until potatoes are tender. Blend remaining tomato sauce into flour until smooth. Slowly stir this into the sauce and cook, stirring, until thickened. Serves 6.

Mamma's Cabbage Patch Stew

1–2 lbs. extra-lean ground beef
1 medium onion, chopped
1 c. diced celery
2 c. finely shredded cabbage
2 c. water
2 Tbsp. Worcestershire sauce

2 tsp. chili powder
2 tsp. salt
2 Tbsp. sugar
1 14.5-oz. can stewed tomatoes, cut up
1 8-oz. can kidney beans

Brown the meat in a large skillet; drain. Add onions, celery, and cabbage; cook until wilted. Add water, Worcestershire sauce, chili powder, salt, and sugar. Add tomatoes and beans. Cover and cook for 30 minutes.

Note from Bev

I always serve this lip-smacking stew piping hot and with a variety of cheeses and specialty crackers.

OYSTER STEW

4 c. whole milk

24 oysters, shucked

2 Tbsp. butter or margarine

Salt and pepper

Bring milk to boil and remove from heat. In a separate saucepan combine the oysters, butter, and salt and pepper to taste. Cover and cook for 3–4 minutes. Remove the lid and add the boiled milk to oysters. Bring to a boil for 1 full minute.

Note from Bev

Very appetizing when served along with buttered toast or grilled cheese sandwiches. Yummy!

Put a pinch of baking soda in tomatoes before adding milk when making tomato soup. This keeps milk from curdling.

PENNSYLVANIA DUTCH CHICKEN CORN SOUP

6 c. chicken broth

2 c. corn (fresh or frozen)

1 c. noodles

1 c. chopped celery

2 Tbsp. chopped parsley

1 tsp. salt (unless broth is already seasoned)

1/4 tsp. freshly ground pepper

2 c. cooked, diced chicken

Bring the broth to a boil; add the corn, noodles, celery, parsley, salt, and pepper. Boil 5 minutes or until corn and noodles are tender. Add chicken and heat through.

Note from Bev

This soup is so hearty and tasty! It's the Pennsylvania Dutch version of chicken noodle soup.

Cauliflower and Broccoli Soup

1 or 2 med. onions, chopped
1 Tbsp. butter
1 qt. water
1 head cauliflower, chopped
1 head broccoli, chopped
1 Tbsp. onion salt
$\frac{1}{4}$ tsp. pepper

$\frac{1}{3}$ c. flour
$\frac{1}{2}$ c. water
1 qt. hot milk
1 pound Velveeta or American cheese, broken into small pieces

Fry onion in butter (just a little); add 1 qt. water, cauliflower, broccoli, onion salt, and pepper. Boil until vegetables are soft; mash with potato masher. Make a paste with flour and $\frac{1}{2}$ c. water and stir into soup. Remove from heat and add hot milk and cheese. Return to stove and heat through until cheese is melted; do not boil. If soup is not salty enough, add regular salt or more onion salt.

Variations: For potato soup, use potatoes instead of cauliflower and broccoli.

For clam chowder, use 6–8 oz. canned clams and omit the cheese, cauliflower, and broccoli.

Too many cooks spoil the broth.

Main Dishes

Mam was smart thataway. There were times when she enticed her daughters to redd up the bedrooms, changing sheets and dusting, with the promise of chicken and dumplings for lunch. "The sooner we finish cleanin', the quicker we'll eat." Mamma's gentle, persuasive prodding taught them by example that work was, indeed, fun.

—from *October Song*

(Note: See REBECCA LAPP'S HOMEMADE DUMPLINGS on page 80.)

AMISH MEAT LOAF

2 lb. ground beef	1/4 tsp. pepper
1 c. cracker crumbs	Flour
1 Tbsp. chopped onion	1 10.75-oz. can cream of
1 c. milk	mushroom soup
1 tsp. salt	1/2 c. steak sauce

Mix first six ingredients together and shape into loaf; refrigerate overnight. Cut loaf into 1/2-inch slices and dip in flour. Brown slightly on both sides; place in casserole dish. Mix cream of mushroom soup with steak sauce; pour over meat loaf. Bake at 250 degrees for 2 hours.

PORK CHOPS WITH RICE

5 pork chops	2 c. strained tomatoes
1/2 c. uncooked rice	1 1/2 tsp. salt
1/2 c. diced green pepper	1/8 tsp. pepper

Fry chops slightly in a hot pan. Move chops to one side and add rice to the fat; allow rice to brown. Push rice to side of pan and finish browning chops. Add pepper, tomatoes, and seasoning. Cover; cook slowly over low heat for 1 hour.

LAMB LOAF

1 lb. ground lamb*	1 tsp. salt
1 c. fine bread crumbs	1 tsp. ground cumin
1/2 c. V8 juice	2 eggs, beaten
1/2 c. water	1 large onion, finely chopped

Mix all ingredients together and put into a glass loaf pan. Bake at 375 degrees for 1 hour.

*May substitute ground beef to make meat loaf.

And he took butter, and milk, and the calf which he had dressed, and set it before them; and he stood by them under the tree, and they did eat. —GENESIS 18:8

DINNER IN A DISH

1 medium onion, minced	3 c. fresh or frozen corn
1 green pepper, minced (optional)	$1/2$ tsp. salt
	Pepper
2 Tbsp. shortening or margarine	2 tomatoes, sliced
1 lb. lean ground beef	1 c. bread crumbs

Sauté onion and green pepper in shortening until tender. Add ground beef; brown. Place a layer of meat into a greased casserole dish. Add a layer of uncooked corn, sprinkle with salt and pepper, and add tomatoes. Repeat layers again, ending with tomato slices. Top with bread crumbs. Bake at 350 degrees for 45 minutes or until bubbly and corn is tender.

Note from Bev

Grandmother Ada was known to "scare up a meal in a hurry." Here's one of the many I especially love to this day.

BAKED SALMON

1 11-oz. can salmon	Dash of salt
$1/2$ c. cooked rice	Dash of pepper
2 eggs	Dash of sugar
2 c. milk	Onion to taste

Mix all ingredients together and press into a greased loaf pan. Bake at 350 degrees for 1 hour.

VEAL RING

Ring:

2 lbs. ground veal	$^1/_8$ tsp. pepper
1 lb. ground pork	1 tsp. mustard
$^1/_4$ c. minced onion	1 tsp. salt
$^1/_4$ c. horseradish	2 eggs
$^1/_2$ tsp. sage	$^1/_2$ c. catsup

Bread sauce:

1 c. milk	$^1/_3$ tsp. pepper
$^1/_3$ c. bread crumbs	$1^1/_2$ Tbsp. butter
$^1/_3$ tsp. salt	1 small onion, finely chopped

Ring: Mix veal and pork together; add onion, horseradish, seasonings, and eggs. Pour catsup in the bottom of a well-greased ring mold. Pack in the meat mixture. Bake at 350 degrees for 1 hour.

When finished baking, turn out catsup side up. Serve with bread sauce.

Bread sauce: Mix together ingredients and bake at 350 degrees for 20 minutes.

But we all, with open face beholding as in a glass the glory of the Lord, are changed into the same image from glory to glory, even as by the Spirit of the Lord.

–2 CORINTHIANS 3:18

SHREDDED CORN BEEF

1 c. shredded corn beef	1 onion, chopped
2 c. peas	1 c. stewed tomatoes

Boil all ingredients together for 1 hour and serve.

Ways to serve beef: in stew, meatloaf, patties, and with gravy.

Macaroni Goulash

Butter and shortening
1/4 c. diced celery
1/4 c. diced onion
1 lb. ground chuck steak or
    lean ground beef

1 10.75-oz. can tomato soup
2 c. cooked macaroni

Melt a pat of butter and a bit of shortening in a large skillet. Add the diced celery and onion; sauté until tender. Brown the hamburger in the sautéed mixture; add tomato soup. Mix together with cooked macaroni and serve hot.

Note from Bev

This dish was the ``talk of the town'' when visiting ministers and their families spent time in Ada's homey kitchen during the Depression years.

Amish Fried Chicken

1 c. crushed saltine crackers
    or bread crumbs
1/4 c. flour
2 tsp. salt
1 tsp. oregano
1/2 tsp. Frontier Veggie pepper*

1/2 tsp. garlic granules or
    garlic powder
2 chickens, cut in pieces
2 eggs, mixed with 1/4 c. water
1 c. water

Combine crackers or bread crumbs, flour, and seasonings. Dip each piece of chicken in egg and water mixture; coat with crumb mixture. Fry quickly in butter until brown. Place chicken pieces in a single layer in roasting pan or 4-qt. casserole dish. Add 1 c. water; cover with foil. Bake at 350 degrees for approximately 90 minutes.

*If Frontier Veggie pepper is unavailable, use mixture of 1/4 t. ground black pepper, 1/4 t. onion salt, 1/4 t. red pepper, and 1/8 t. celery seed.

BAKED MACARONI AND CHEESE

4 c. uncooked macaroni

5 Tbsp. butter

1/3 c. flour

2 rounded tsp. salt

2 rounded tsp. dry mustard

5 c. milk

10 oz. sharp Cheddar cheese, cut in pieces

10 oz. extra-sharp white cheese, cut in pieces

Bring large pot of salted water to a boil; slowly add macaroni. Boil for 10 minutes, stirring occasionally. Drain; place macaroni in a buttered 4-quart glass baking dish.

While macaroni is boiling, melt butter in another saucepan. Remove pan from heat; blend in flour, salt, and mustard. Return to heat and gradually add milk, stirring constantly, until sauce thickens and is smooth. Bring to a boil. Carefully add cheese pieces to boiling milk mixture, stirring until all cheese is melted. Pour cheese mixture over cooked macaroni; mix evenly. Bake at 350 degrees for 45 minutes or until golden brown and bubbly.

RICE AND EGGS FOR TWO

1/3 c. uncooked enriched converted long-grain rice

1 Tbsp. olive oil

1 c. water

1/2 large white onion, chopped

1/4 tsp. salt

2 eggs

In saucepan, fry rice in olive oil until golden brown, stirring constantly. Add water, onion, and salt. Cover pan and bring to a boil. Simmer for 20 minutes, stirring about every 5 minutes. Add a bit of water if needed. Top each serving with an egg "over light." Mix all together, adding salt to taste. Serve immediately.

Note from Bev

A nice alternative for a light lunch or can be served as an appetizer.

Tuna Casserole

1 6.5-oz. can tuna, drained
1 3-oz. can french fried onions
1 c. thinly sliced celery
¼ tsp. onion powder

4 oz. canned or fresh mushrooms, sliced
1 10.75-oz. can cream of
  celery soup

Combine tuna and ½ can fried onions with remaining ingredients; place in greased casserole dish. Bake at 350 degrees for 25 minutes. Sprinkle remaining onions on top; bake for 5 more minutes.

Ruth's Elegant Chicken

8 boneless chicken breasts
16 slices boiled ham
4 oz. dried beef
1 c. sour cream

1 10.75-oz. can cream of
  mushroom soup
Paprika

Cut chicken breasts in half; wrap each half with a slice of ham. Cover bottom of baking dish with dried beef; place chicken breasts on top. Blend together sour cream and cream of mushroom soup; pour over chicken. Sprinkle with paprika. Bake at 375 degrees for 60–75 minutes, covered; uncover and bake 15 minutes longer.

Rebecca Lapp's Homemade Dumplings

1 c. sifted flour
1 tsp. salt

2 tsp. baking powder
1 egg, beaten

Mix together dry ingredients; pour beaten egg over mixture. Add drops of cold tap water, but be careful not to get too much! Stir together. Drop by big spoonfuls into a deep pot of simmering chicken stew, as dumplings tend to boil up. (Or simply place dumplings in boiling water for 5 minutes.) Either way, boil for 5 minutes without lifting lid. Serve dumplings in stew or gravy or with cooked chicken.

TURKEY LOAF

1 egg
1 c. whole milk
1 lb. skinless ground turkey

6 slices white bread, cubed
1/2 c. chopped celery
1/4 c. chopped onion

Beat egg and milk with a fork. Mix together with remaining ingredients and press into loaf pan. Bake at 350 degrees for 1 hour.

Note from Bev

If mixture seems too moist, sprinkle a few dried bread crumbs on top. Sure to satisfy!

CHICKEN CASSEROLE

6 Tbsp. butter
6 Tbsp. flour
3 c. chicken broth
1/2 tsp. salt
3/4 tsp. celery salt
1 10.75-oz. can cream of chicken soup

1 10.75-oz. can cream of celery soup
8 oz. Velveeta cheese (cut up)
1 12-oz. pkg. noodles, cooked
4 c. diced cooked chicken
Dry stuffing mix

In a saucepan, melt butter over medium-low heat. Stir flour in slowly, using a wire whisk, until the butter and flour mixture begins to bubble. Continue cooking and stirring for about two minutes; remove from heat.

In a separate pan, heat chicken broth; stir in salt and celery salt. Once broth is fully heated, add it to the butter and flour mixture, stirring quickly. Return the saucepan to heat; stir over medium heat until sauce begins to thicken (don't allow it to boil). Add soups and Velveeta cheese; cook until creamy and smooth. Mix sauce, noodles, and chicken together; pour into greased 9×13 casserole pan and cover with stuffing mix. Bake at 300 degrees for 1 hour. Makes 8–10 servings.

Cooked at low temperatures, meats shrink less. This also provides more broth and better flavor.

Amish Roast[1]

1 5-7 lb. chicken, 8-10 lb. capon, or 12–15 lb. turkey (if using a turkey, make a double batch of stuffing)

Stuffing:

3 cups chopped celery

1–3 c. chopped onion (to taste)

1 c. butter

1 Tbsp. shortening

1½ gal. bread cubes (approximately 24 cups—use 2 24-oz. loaves white bread)

4 eggs

1 tsp. salt

¼ rounded tsp. pepper

Pinch of lemon pepper

Pinch of Spike seasoning

Pinch of Mrs. Dash seasoning

Pinch of Italian seasoning

1 Tbsp. olive oil

Fry celery and onion in butter and shortening until tender; toss lightly with the bread cubes. Beat eggs; mix in seasonings and olive oil. Pour over bread cubes. Mix well and stuff chicken, capon, or turkey.

For chicken, bake in a covered roaster at 325 degrees for 2½ to 3¼ hours.* For capon, bake in a covered roaster at 325 degrees for 2½ to 3¼ hours, checking for doneness after 3 hours.* For turkey, bake in a covered roaster at 300 degrees for 8 hours or overnight.* Bake extra stuffing in a covered casserole dish at 325 degrees for 1 hour.

*Alternative: Bird may be baked in Reynolds Oven Bag according to directions in box.

When chicken, capon, or turkey is done, remove from oven and let

---

[1]The "roast" is the mixture of stuffing and finely chopped meat.

sit, covered, for 30 minutes—meat will be more moist. Set broth aside and cool. After 30 minutes, remove meat from bones. Grind the skin in a meat grinder and mix in with cooked stuffing. Chop meat in very small pieces—the smaller the better—and mix in with cooked stuffing.

After broth is cool, remove "fat" layer from the top and reserve for when the stuffing is reheated; reserve broth for making gravy (see recipe below). Spread fat over the top of the stuffing mixture when reheating. Reheat stuffing and meat mixture in a 4-qt. covered greased casserole dish at 325 degrees for 45 minutes to 1 hour, checking center for doneness before serving.

Note: Make several days ahead of time. The flavor gets through better this way.

Note from Bev

On Christmas morning, the Buchwalter kitchen was always "redd up" first and everyone dressed for the day before they gathered in the front room for family worship. After prayer and Bible reading, Mother, her seven siblings, and their parents presented simple gifts to one another, often homemade. Before sitting down to dinner they joined their voices in song with a rousing "Joy to the World."

GRAVY FOR AMISH ROAST

Place 1 c. flour in a small bowl and gradually stir in enough water to form a smooth paste. Add some turkey or chicken broth into flour/water mixture until it is a "watery" consistency so the gravy doesn't get lumpy as additional flour is added. Simmer gravy until thickened to desired consistency, adding more flour if needed and stirring to keep smooth. Add salt to taste if needed.

Practice makes perfect.

HOMEMADE HAMBURGER HELPER

1 lb. ground beef

2 10.75-oz. cans tomato soup

4 soup cans of water

2 c. uncooked macaroni

1 can peas and carrots, drained

Brown the ground beef; add both cans of tomato soup, 2 cans water, and the macaroni. Cook until macaroni is soft, adding the other 2 cans of water as needed when cooking, stirring occasionally. When macaroni is soft, stir in peas and carrots; remove from heat. Let mixture sit for about 15 minutes to thicken.

PORK CHOPS

4 pork chops

¼ c. butter, melted

3 c. soft bread crumbs

2 Tbsp. chopped onion

¼ c. water

¼ tsp. poultry seasoning

1 10.75-oz. can cream of mushroom soup

½ c. milk

Brown pork chops on both sides in melted butter; place in un-greased casserole dish. Mix bread crumbs, onion, water, and poultry seasoning together; place a mound of "stuffing" on each pork chop. Blend cream of mushroom soup with milk; pour over chops and stuffing. Bake, uncovered, at 350 degrees for 1 hour.

CHICKEN AND WAFFLES

Make waffles. Mix 2 Tbsp. cornstarch with water until dissolved. Add cornstarch mixture to chicken broth or gravy containing small pieces of chicken; thicken. Pour over waffles.

Make hay while the sun shines.

A good name is rather to be chosen than great riches, and loving favour rather than silver and gold. —PROVERBS 22:1

AMISH HAYSTACKS

1 box Ritz crackers, crushed

1 28-oz. box Minute Rice, cooked

8 lbs. ground beef, browned, mixed with spaghetti sauce and taco seasoning mix*

Choice of toppings: chopped tomatoes (8), green peppers (oodles), grated carrots (lots), raisins (mounds), black and green olives (plenty), walnuts (many), onions (several diced), sunflower seeds (an ample amount), and salsa (several jars)

Stack ingredients on plates in layers, using cracker crumbs first, then rice, followed by ground beef. The order of the other ingredients is not important. Top with grated cheddar cheese or cheddar cheese soup.

*Use approximately 1 package taco seasoning per pound of ground beef and four large cans spaghetti sauce, adjusting to taste.

Note from Bev

Talk about feeding a multitude! This recipe is commonly used at fundraiser dinners in Amish and Mennonite communities. Quite tasty, and additional condiments can be added (or deleted) to suit your taste buds. The meal is not only delicious but very filling.

CREAMED CHIPPED BEEF

Melt 2 Tbsp. butter in a skillet; stir in 2 Tbsp. flour and mix well. Add 2 c. milk and 1 c. chipped beef cut up in tiny pieces. Stir well until hot and thickened. Pour over waffles or mashed potatoes.

RICE PILAF TURKEY STUFFING

½ c. pine nuts or slivered almonds	½ c. chopped parsley or celery
½ c. butter	¼ tsp. allspice
1 c. finely chopped onion	2 tsp. salt
3 c. uncooked long-grain rice	¼ tsp. pepper
¼ tsp. cinnamon	5 c. chicken broth

Toast nuts in 350-degree oven for 5 minutes. In a wide frying pan, heat butter and sauté onion for about 5 minutes. Add rice and cook, stirring, over medium heat for 4 minutes. Blend in cinnamon, parsley, allspice, salt, pepper, and toasted nuts.

In another pan, boil broth and pour over rice mixture; stir lightly. Cover and reduce heat to low. Simmer until moisture is absorbed (about 25 minutes).

EASY CHICKEN DIJON

2 16-oz. pkgs. broccoli spears, cooked	½ c. grated cheese (optional)
2 c. diced cooked chicken	1 tsp. lemon juice
1 10.75-oz. can cream of chicken soup	¼ tsp. curry powder
⅔ c. mayonnaise	1 4-oz. can mushrooms
	1 c. croutons, cereal, or bread crumbs for topping

Place broccoli spears in a greased casserole dish, layering with pieces of chicken. Combine remaining ingredients except for croutons, cereal, or bread crumbs; mix well. Pour sauce over broccoli and chicken; sprinkle with topping. Bake at 350 degrees for 30–45 minutes or until bubbly.

Early to bed and early to rise, makes a man healthy, wealthy, and wise.
—*Benjamin Franklin*

FISH À LA WORCESTER

1½ lb. halibut, flounder, or cod fillets
3½ tsp. Worcestershire sauce, divided
½ c. melted margarine
½ c. soft bread crumbs
¼ c. finely minced onion

¼ c. finely minced green pepper
¼ c. finely minced red pepper
¼ tsp. salt
¼ tsp. minced garlic
Parsley sprigs

Sauce:

2 Tbsp. melted butter
1 tsp. Worcestershire sauce
1 tsp. lemon juice
½ c. sour cream

¼ c. grated Cheddar cheese
Salt and pepper to taste
Paprika to top

Fish: Preheat broiler to 500 degrees. Wash fish and place on ungreased pan. Brush fillets with ½ tsp. Worcestershire sauce. Set aside. In small bowl combine margarine, crumbs, onion, green and red peppers, salt, garlic, and remaining Worcestershire sauce. Spread mixture over fish.

Broil 6 inches from heat until fish "flakes" easily when tested with a fork. Arrange fish on heated platter; top with sauce and garnish with parsley. Serves 4.

Sauce: Blend melted butter with Worcestershire sauce, lemon juice, sour cream, and grated cheese in a small saucepan. Stir continually until sauce is smooth and thick. Add salt and pepper to taste; sprinkle with paprika.

Note from Bev

Sauce is great on halibut steaks, flounder, perch, and fillets of white fish.

Baked Shad

Place 3 or 4 slices of bacon in a roaster. Cut the shad in half, lengthwise, and lay in roaster with skin side down. Dot with butter and salt generously. Spread evenly with 2 Tbsp. milk. Bake for 45 minutes at 350 degrees. Top with dressing (below).

Dressing:

1 c. whole milk, warmed
1 level tsp. flour, moistened
  with a bit of water

Butter, pepper, and salt to
  taste

Simmer dressing ingredients together and spread on meat.

Note from Bev

My dad recalls shad as being a popular "catch" with our friends in Quarryville, Pa. (Shad fish travel in large schools in the Susquehanna River.) Be careful when eating this baked fish, akin to herring, as there are often small bones.

Chicken and Broccoli Quiche

3 Tbsp. butter
1 small onion, chopped
3 Tbsp. flour
1¼ c. milk
3 eggs, beaten
1 unbaked pie shell

¾ c. cubed cooked chicken
¾ c. chopped cooked broccoli
Dash of basil
Salt
Grated cheese

Sauté onions in butter until transparent. Stir in flour until thick; add milk and blend. Add eggs and stir but do not cook. Pour mixture into unbaked pie shell; add chicken, broccoli, a dash of basil, and salt to taste. Top with grated cheese. Bake at 350 degrees for 40 minutes. Serve hot.

Note from Bev

This dish is really satisfying and so delicious!

TURKEY CASSEROLE

1½ c. milk
1 10.75-oz. can cream of
mushroom soup
3 eggs, beaten
2¼ c. uncooked fine egg
noodles

2–2½ c. cooked, cubed turkey
1 c. shredded sharp American
cheese
¼ c. chopped green pepper
2 Tbsp. chopped pimiento
⅓ c. grated Parmesan cheese

Blend milk into soup. Stir in remaining ingredients except Parmesan cheese. Pour into shallow baking dish; top with Parmesan cheese. Bake at 350 degrees for 30 minutes or until a knife inserted in center comes out clean.

Prove all things; hold fast that which is good. Abstain from all appearance of evil. —I THESSALONIANS 5:21–22

CHICKEN MUSHROOM BAKE

⅓ c. flour
1 tsp. salt
½ tsp. pepper
1 tsp. paprika
2–3 c. cubed chicken
⅓ c. butter

1 10.75-oz. can cream of
mushroom soup
1 c. sour cream
½ c. sliced mushrooms
⅔ c. shredded Cheddar cheese

Combine flour, salt, pepper, and paprika in a paper bag. Shake chicken in flour mixture. Melt butter in large skillet and brown chicken on all sides. Place in a 9×13 baking dish. Combine soup, sour cream, and mushrooms; pour over chicken. Bake at 350 degrees for 1 hour or until chicken is tender. Sprinkle with cheese and return to oven until cheese is melted.

TUNA MELTS

3 or 4 Tbsp. light olive oil

6-oz. can of tuna

1/4 large white onion, chopped

1/4 tsp. salt (or to taste)

10 oz. Swiss cheese

4 pieces bread, buttered on one side

Garlic granules or garlic powder (optional)

Put approximately 1 Tbsp. olive oil in a small cast-iron frying pan; add the tuna, chopped onion, and salt. Cook on medium-low heat until tuna is lightly browned and onion is tender.

Thinly slice the cheese, cutting enough slices to cover each piece of bread. Heat large cast-iron frying pan for 10 to 15 seconds, then turn the heat off. Put 2 or 3 Tbsp. oil in the pan. Sprinkle some garlic granules on the buttered side of 2 pieces of the bread, then put them buttered side down in the oil. Place cheese slices on each, then put half of hot tuna mixture on each slice of bread. Place remaining cheese slices over the top of the hot tuna mixture, then cover with the remaining pieces of bread, buttered side up. Sprinkle garlic granules on the bread. Cover the pan and fry on medium heat for approximately 3–5 minutes on the first side, or until golden brown. Turn sandwiches and fry on the second side for 1–2 minutes, or until golden brown. (Second side gets brown much quicker because the pan is already hot.) Makes 2 tuna melts.

Note: These instructions are for a gas stove; the heating times may vary a bit for an electric one.

GRANDMOTHER BUCHWALTER'S MEAT LOAF

1 lb. lean ground beef

1 tsp. salt

1 c. bread crumbs

1 c. milk

1 egg, beaten

Finely chopped onions to taste

Mix all ingredients thoroughly; place in loaf pan. Bake at 350 degrees for 1 hour.

Vegetables and Side Dishes

A careful look at her pantry—each shelf lined with freshly canned vegetables, fruit, and preserves—and she spied parsley and ground pepper needed for her scalloped potatoes recipe, as well as some coconut and nutmeg for the coconut squash dish. Her eyes caught sight of a row of tall glass jars of asparagus and she decided, then and there, to add creamed asparagus to her menu for Saturday night. She also planned to make Mary's lime salad, a recipe from their teen years, which called for marshmallows and cream cheese, two ingredients she had written on her list. She would make sure she squeezed in a quick trip to the grocery store sometime today for those items.

—from *October Song*

(Note: See SCALLOPED POTATOES WITH CHEESE SAUCE on page 96.)

AMISH BROCCOLI DISH

2 10-oz. bags frozen chopped
  broccoli
4 oz. Velveeta cheese
1 10.75-oz. can cream of
  mushroom soup

$1/2$ tsp. salt
2 c. crushed croutons
5 Tbsp. melted butter

Boil and drain broccoli. Cream together cheese and cream of mushroom soup; mix in broccoli and salt. Place in greased 3-qt. casserole dish. Mix croutons and melted butter together and pour evenly on top of casserole. Bake at 350 degrees for 20 minutes.

Note from Bev

Another wonderful-good Amish recipe—the ultimate way to describe it.

JANE'S CELERY CASSEROLE

4 c. diced celery
$1/4$ c. slivered almonds
$1/2$ c. sliced water chestnuts
5 Tbsp. butter, divided
3 Tbsp. flour

1 c. chicken broth
$3/4$ c. half-and-half cream
$1/2$ c. canned mushrooms
$1/2$ c. grated Parmesan cheese
$1/2$ c. dry bread crumbs

Boil celery for 5 minutes; celery should still be crisp. Drain and place into a greased 1.5-qt. baking dish with almonds and water chestnuts. Melt 3 Tbsp. butter. Add flour; stir and cook for a few minutes over low heat. Slowly stir in broth with half-and-half. Simmer over low heat for 5 minutes. Add mushrooms to sauce, then pour over celery. Sprinkle with Parmesan cheese and dot with remaining 2 Tbsp. of butter. Finish with bread crumbs. Bake at 350 degrees until bubbly, approximately 30 minutes.

SWEET POTATOES DELUXE

2 c. cooked, mashed sweet
potatoes
3 Tbsp. butter or margarine
½ tsp. salt

Scant pinch of pepper
1 egg, beaten
Corn flakes cereal
Olive oil

To mashed sweet potatoes, add butter, salt, pepper, and egg; mix well. Shape into small balls and roll in crushed corn flakes. Fry sweet potato balls in olive oil and drain. If sweet potatoes become too dry before shaping into balls, simply add hot milk to moisten.

ASPARAGUS CASSEROLE

2 8-oz. cans or 1 15.5-oz. can
asparagus
4 hard-boiled eggs, sliced

1 10.75-oz. can cream of
chicken soup
Crumble of potato chips

In a greased 2-qt. casserole dish, place asparagus, eggs, and cream of chicken soup. Top with crumbled chips. Bake at 350 degrees for 45 minutes.

*Put salt water on cabbage or spinach
to drive out bugs or worms.*

GREEN BEANS THE PENNSYLVANIA DUTCH WAY

Cook green beans until just tender to fork. In a small frying pan, put 2 or 3 Tbsp. of flour; stir constantly. When flour is light brown, stir in ¼ c. butter and ½ c. whole milk. Pour over beans and serve.

Note from Bev

I never tire of this delicious way to cook and serve green beans. It's one of those tried and true dishes you'll see at oodles of gatherings in and around Lancaster County.

BEETS

1 32-oz. can beets (1 qt.)	$^3/_4$ tsp. salt (or to taste)
2 Tbsp. butter	$^1/_2$ c. sugar
2 rounded Tbsp. flour	Juice of 1 orange

Drain beets, reserving juice. Set aside. Melt butter in saucepan; mix in flour, salt, and sugar. Add the juice of the orange, then add reserved beet juice very gradually. Simmer until thickened. Add beets last. Serve.

Note from Bev

Incredibly delicious, and the ideal side for a luncheon or a lighter meal.

Everything in life only lasts for a season.

SPINACH CASSEROLE

3 Tbsp. butter	$^1/_4$ tsp. pepper
3 Tbsp. chopped onion	$^1/_4$ tsp. nutmeg
1 lb. mushrooms, finely chopped	2 c. half-and-half cream
3 Tbsp. flour	3 10-oz. pkgs. frozen spinach, thawed
2 tsp. salt	$^1/_4$ c. grated Swiss cheese

Sauté onions and mushrooms in butter until transparent. Blend in flour, salt, pepper, and nutmeg. Gradually add in the half-and-half and stir until thick. In a well-buttered baking dish, spread half the uncooked spinach. Cover with half of the mushroom sauce. Repeat layers. Bake at 350 degrees for 15 minutes. Sprinkle the cheese on top and return to oven until cheese is melted.

BAKED BEANS

1 lb. dry pinto beans

½ tsp. prepared mustard

½ onion, diced

1 14-oz. bottle catsup

⅛ c. brown sugar

½ lb. smoked meat, chopped

¼ tsp. pepper

3 Tbsp. vinegar

Cook beans in Dutch oven until soft. Add the remaining ingredients, including smoked meat. Bake, covered, at 350 degrees for one hour.

SCALLOPED POTATOES WITH CHEESE SAUCE

3 Tbsp. mild Cheddar cheese, grated

3 Tbsp. butter or margarine

1 tsp. salt

2 Tbsp. flour

2½ c. whole milk

6 large potatoes

2 Tbsp. minced white onion

1 c. diced cooked ham or 1 c. fried bacon pieces for flavor

Additional butter

Pepper to taste

1 tsp. dried parsley

Melt cheese and butter in a saucepan on low heat. When melted, add salt and flour. Continue cooking until smooth. Add milk gradually, stirring until well blended. Cook until thickened.

Pare and thinly slice potatoes. In a greased casserole dish, make a layer of potatoes and sprinkle with part of the minced onion and part of the diced ham or bacon pieces. Repeat layers until all ingredients are used.

Pour the melted cheese and butter mixture over the layers. Dot with butter; sprinkle with pepper and dried parsley. Bake, covered, for one hour at 375 degrees. Uncover and continue baking for approximately 10–15 minutes or until top layer forms a brown crust.

Let your speech be alway with grace, seasoned with salt.

—COLOSSIANS 4:6

Dried Corn Casserole

1/2 c. milk

2 eggs, beaten

1 c. dried sweet corn, previ-
ously soaked in 1 c. hot milk
(I use Cope's toasted dried
sweet corn)

2 Tbsp. butter

2 Tbsp. sugar

1 tsp. salt

Dash of pepper

Mix all ingredients together; place in a buttered baking dish. Bake at 375 degrees for 40 minutes.

Note from Bev

Dried corn is unique to Lancaster County and has a much different flavor than fresh corn, canned, or frozen. Pennsylvania Dutch cooks toast the corn in woodstoves. The process caramelizes the natural sugars, giving it a slightly nutty flavor. I remember enjoying this casserole from early childhood when Mother served it at Thanksgiving and Christmas Day dinners. My Swedish husband, however, has been known to season dried corn with catsup! An interesting and tasty twist, to say the least.

Scalloped Asparagus

3 c. fresh asparagus, trimmed,
tips reserved

4 hard-boiled eggs, chopped

1/4 c. flour

1 c. milk

1/4 c. butter

1/2 c. grated cheese

1 c. bread crumbs

Put half of asparagus in greased casserole dish; place eggs on top. Combine flour, milk, and butter; pour onto asparagus and eggs. Add grated cheese and bread crumbs. Dress with asparagus tips. Brown at 425 degrees for 20 minutes.

Baked Potatoes

Prepare 1 baked potato per person.

Poke skin of baking potatoes (Idaho, red potatoes, etc.) with fork 4 times and coat with olive oil; sprinkle with salt. Place on a cookie sheet or put foil on the rack below the potatoes, as the oil may drip just a bit. Bake on center rack at 375 degrees for 1 hour (longer for larger potatoes). When done, potato should be fairly soft when jabbed with a fork. After potatoes are baked, allow to sit a couple minutes before cutting open. Then, being careful not to burn your fingers, quickly and gently push all around, or squeeze the potato to soften the inside. Cut open and serve with butter, sour cream, and salt.

Optional: Serve with snipped chives and grated cheese.

Home is home,
be it never so homely.
—Old English Proverb

Amanda's Tomato Zucchini Casserole

1 lb. zucchini	1½ tsp. salt
2 medium onions, thinly sliced	¼ tsp. black pepper
5 medium tomatoes, sliced	1 c. grated cheese
¾ c. fine dry bread crumbs	

Wash but do not peel zucchini. Cut into ⅛-inch slices, then cook in boiling salted water for 5 minutes and drain. In a buttered casserole dish, arrange alternate layers of zucchini, onions, tomatoes, bread crumbs, and seasoning. Top with tomato slices. Cover and bake at 400 degrees for 1 hour. Remove cover and sprinkle with cheese. Return to oven until cheese is melted.

Note from Bev

Mm-m, good!

DELICIOUS BAKED SWEET POTATOES

Bake sweet potatoes in oven at 375 degrees for 45–60 minutes (depending on size of potato). Place foil on rack underneath the potatoes, as juices may ooze during baking time. Bake until soft when jabbed with fork. Cut open and mash with fork. Cover with butter and salt, then add brown sugar to taste.

SUSANNA'S CREAMY CABBAGE

4 c. shredded cabbage	1 c. milk
$\frac{1}{2}$ c. water	1 tsp. salt
2 Tbsp. flour	$\frac{1}{8}$ tsp. pepper

Cook cabbage in water for 5 minutes. Sprinkle flour over cabbage; mix well. Add remaining ingredients and cook, stirring occasionally, until thickened.

BAKED CORN

8 Tbsp. butter	$\frac{1}{4}$ tsp. ground black pepper
7–8 cups frozen corn, thawed (excellent if frozen fresh)	24 saltine crackers, crushed
	4 eggs
2 Tbsp. sugar	2 c. milk
2 tsp. salt (rounded)	

Melt butter in large saucepan. Add corn, sugar, salt, and pepper; heat through. Add crushed crackers. Beat eggs and milk together and add to corn mixture; heat to almost boiling. Pour into buttered 9×13 glass baking dish. Bake at 350 degrees for 50 minutes or until lightly browned.

Add a little milk to water in which cauliflower is cooking; the cauliflower will remain attractively white.

BROWNED BUTTER

Melt 1 regular stick of real butter (not unsalted) in a watched skillet until brown. Stir with dry fork, as water will make the butter "spritz" (spit). Drizzle browned butter over corn, carrots, peas, lima beans, green beans, mashed potatoes, noodles, or stewed crackers. May also be spread over bread crumbs for stuffing.

Note from Bev

Browned butter can be used on almost any vegetable imaginable and is uniquely Pennsylvania Dutch. Very tasty and makes for a pretty presentation.

MASHED POTATOES

5 lb. potatoes, peeled and quartered
3 tsp. salt, divided
3 Tbsp. butter
2 c. milk, heated
¼ c. butter, browned
Sour cream and/or cream cheese (optional)

In large saucepan, nearly cover potatoes with water. Add 1 tsp. salt to the water and bring to a boil, then simmer until potatoes are soft enough to mash easily. Pour off all water. Mash well, then add 3 Tbsp. butter and mash. Add remaining salt and milk, ½ cup at a time, mashing well after each addition. Pour hot browned butter over the top. Serve immediately with gravy.

To reheat leftovers:
(1) Add a bit of sour cream and/or cream cheese and milk.
(2) Make potato cakes by patting refrigerated mashed potatoes into a small flat "cake" and frying on both sides until dark golden brown. Serve with "eggs over light."

"A Friend Indeed" (excerpt)
–Dedicated to the memory of Edna Keller

A cook par excellence—few could compare,
Though I'm sure there are some who would try.
Edna's feasts were like a country fair,
When you thought you were finished,
She'd serve you the pie!
She was a "Martha"—extremely hospitable,
Anyone knows who has sat at her table!
But a "Mary" she was in her heart,
As she chose the better part.
Because she loved God's Holy Word,
Edna is now forever with the Lord.
She was loving and giving,
In the true sense of the word.
Ever cheerful, diligent, and faithful . . .
Living a life that wholly pleased our Lord.
—Jane Buchwalter Jones

Note from Bev

My mother wrote this poem on the day of Edna's heavenly homegoing. She was "Aunt Edna" to my sister and me for as long as I can remember. Aunt Edna made the best mashed potatoes, and I was always eager to help her by licking off the beaters when we were invited for Sunday dinner.

MARBLE MASHED POTATOES

2 lb. sweet potatoes, peeled
and chunked

2 lb. white potatoes, peeled
and chunked

8 oz. cream cheese, divided

Cook potatoes in separate pots until soft enough to mash. Drain, saving ¾ c. cooking water from each potato pot. Mash potatoes and sweet potatoes, adding 4 ounces cream cheese to each. Add cooking water, salt, and pepper to taste. Spoon potatoes, alternating each kind, into shallow 2½-quart microwave-safe dish. Lightly mix with tip of fork. Either bake at 350 degrees, covered, for 40 minutes to 1 hour, or microwave on high for 8 minutes. Potatoes can be refrigerated up to 2 days.

Let nothing be done through strife or vainglory; but in low-liness of mind let each esteem other better than themselves.

–PHILIPPIANS 2:3

CORN PUDDING

1 c. fresh or frozen corn

2 c. milk

2–4 eggs, slightly beaten

2 Tbsp. sugar

1 Tbsp. flour

Butter and salt to taste

Soak corn in milk for 1 hour. Mix in the remaining ingredients. Bake in moderate oven—350 degrees—for 45 minutes or until a table knife inserted near the center of the pudding comes out clean.

Note: Omit flour or add more eggs if desired.

GRANDMA FISHER'S OYSTER FILLING

2 12-oz. jars oysters, undrained	Dash pepper
3 c. milk	4 c. flat 6-sided oyster crackers
¾ tsp. salt	½ c. browned butter

Place oysters with their juice, milk, salt, and pepper in a saucepan. Heat just to boiling, then immediately remove from heat. Butter a 4-qt. (covered) baking dish. Layer oyster crackers and oyster/milk mixture. Crackers will float, so gently push them into the milk, distributing oysters as evenly as possible. Bake, covered, at 325 degrees for 1 hour. Drizzle with browned butter before serving.

A pint's a pound the world around.

STEWED CRACKERS

30 saltine crackers	¼ c. butter, browned
2¼ c. scalded milk	

Place saltine crackers in an ungreased 1½-pt. covered baking dish. Pour scalded milk on top of crackers, gently pressing them into milk. Cover and let sit for 10 minutes or put in the oven at 300 degrees for 30 minutes to keep warm. Pour browned butter on top, cutting down through mixture so the browned butter gets mixed through. Makes 4 servings.

NOODLES AND BUTTER

Cook 16 oz. noodles in water until soft; drain. Melt ¼ c. of butter in frying pan until slightly brown. Add noodles and cut up fresh parsley. Mix and serve.

Note from Bev

My sister, Barbara, and I often asked for seconds of this mouth-watering dish when we were girls.

SOUR CREAM SALMON MOLD

1 Tbsp. unflavored gelatin

1/2 c. cold water

1 envelope sour cream sauce mix

1/2 c. mayonnaise

2 tsp. lemon juice

1/4 tsp. dried dillweed

1 16-oz. can salmon

1/2 c. diced celery

Carrot curls or tomato slices

Soften gelatin in cold water, stirring over boiling water until gelatin dissolves; cool. Prepare sour cream sauce according to package directions. Blend in mayonnaise, lemon juice, and dillweed; gradually stir in gelatin. Drain salmon, discarding skin and large bones. Fold salmon and celery into sour cream mixture; turn into a 3-cup mold. Chill until set—4 to 5 hours. Unmold; then garnish with carrot curls or tomato slices. Serves 4.

FARMER'S RICE

1 1/2 c. flour

1 small egg

3 1/2 c. milk

1/2 c. sugar

1 tsp. vanilla

Cinnamon (optional)

Add egg to flour. Mix together and form small rivels by rubbing the mixture between your hands. Stir rivels into almost boiling milk. Boil 5 minutes, stirring constantly. Add sugar and vanilla plus cinnamon if desired.

Note from Bev

An inexpensive dish to make, but it is filling and "sticks to the bones." Farmers' wives used this recipe to stretch their food budget, especially during the Depression, I'm told.

Desserts

Leah and Sadie had dressed for bed rather quickly, accompanied by their usual comments, speaking in quiet tones of the ordinary events of the day, of having especially enjoyed Mamma's supper of barbecued chicken, scalloped potatoes with cheese sauce, fried cucumbers, lima beans, and lemon bars with homemade ice cream for dessert.

—from *The Betrayal*

(Note: see LEMON BARS on page 107.)

Lemon Bars

½ c. butter
1 c. flour
½ c. pecans, chopped
1 c. powdered sugar
8 oz. cream cheese, softened

1¾ c. whipped cream, divided
2 small boxes instant lemon
   pudding mix
3 c. milk
Nuts, optional

Melt butter; mix with flour and pecans. Press into a 9×13 pan. Bake at 350 degrees for 15 minutes. Cool.

Mix together powdered sugar, cream cheese, and 1 c. whipped cream; spread over cooled crust. Blend lemon pudding mix and milk until thick; spread over the cream cheese layer.

Spread remaining whipped cream over mixture. Nuts can be sprinkled on top if desired. Cover and refrigerate. Cut into bars when chilled.

Angels' Salad

1 20-oz. can pineapple
1 large can white cherries
¼ lb. small marshmallows
¼ lb. slivered almonds
2 c. whipped cream

1 c. milk
1 tsp. cornstarch
1 egg, beaten
2 Tbsp. vinegar

Combine all ingredients except for vinegar in saucepan; cook. Remove from heat; stir in vinegar. Cool. Chill in refrigerator for 2–4 hours before serving.

Note from Bev

Sweets for the sweet . . . from Grandma Ada's wooden recipe box to you!

We came unto the land whither thou sentest us, and surely it floweth with milk and honey; and this is the fruit of it.

—NUMBERS 13:27

FROSTED CAROB BROWNIES

Brownies:

1¼ Tbsp. butter

⅔ c. light oil

¾ c. carob powder, divided (sifted after measuring)

2 c. raw sugar (sifted before measuring)

5 eggs

2½ tsp. vanilla

1 c. unbleached flour (sifted after measuring)

Icing:

¾ c. creamy peanut butter

6 Tbsp. carob powder, sifted

½ c. honey

5–6 Tbsp. milk

Brownies: Spray saucepan with olive oil cooking spray, then melt butter. Add oil and ¼ c. carob powder; heat only until mixed and barely at a boil. Mix in sugar. Beat eggs slightly; add eggs and vanilla to mixture in saucepan; mix just until smooth. Mix in flour and remaining carob powder. Bake in a greased and floured 9×13 cake pan at 325 degrees for 30 minutes if glass pan, 350 degrees for 30 minutes if metal pan. Ice brownies immediately after removing from oven.

Icing: Mix peanut butter, carob powder, and honey together. Gradually add milk; mix well. Immediately after spreading icing on brownies, before icing sets, swirls may be added with the tip of a smooth table knife.

Pretzels are often served with ice cream.

Fruity Dessert

Mash ½ c. each of strawberries, raspberries, and sliced peaches. Cut ½ c. marshmallows into small pieces and add to fruit. Beat 1 c. cream until stiff; mix together with fruit and marshmallows. Sweeten to taste.

Chocolate Crunch Surprise

1 c. sugar
1 c. light corn syrup
1 c. peanut butter
6 cups Rice Krispies
½ c. peanuts

1 6-oz. pkg. semisweet choco-
    late chips
1 6-oz. pkg. butterscotch
    morsels

Mix together sugar and light corn syrup; bring to a boil in a 3-qt. saucepan. Remove from heat; blend in the peanut butter, Rice Krispies, and peanuts. Press into a buttered 9×13 pan. Melt chocolate chips and butterscotch morsels over very hot (but not boiling) water. Spread over top of cereal mixture. Chill for 5 minutes or until top is firm. Cut into squares.

Two heads are better than one.

Berry Tapioca

Crush 2 c. fresh berries and sweeten to taste. Set aside. Combine 5 Tbsp. minute tapioca, ½ c. sugar, ¼ tsp. salt, and 2 c. water in top of a double boiler. Place over rapidly boiling water, bring to scalding point and cook about 5 minutes, stirring frequently. Remove from heat. Add berries, 1 Tbsp. lemon juice, and 1 tsp. butter. Chill. Serve with whipped cream and whole berries.

CREAM PUFFS

Puffs:

1 c. water

2 pinches of salt

$1/2$ c. shortening

1 c. flour

3 eggs

Creamed filling:

$1/4$ c. flour

$2/3$ c. sugar

$1/4$ tsp. salt

2 eggs, beaten

$1^1/2$ c. scalded whole milk

2 tsp. vanilla

1 c. heavy cream, whipped (or whipped topping)

Puffs: Bring water to a boil; add shortening and salt. Stir until the mixture returns to a boil. Add all the flour at once. Stir heartily until the mixture pulls away from the side of the pan. Add one unbeaten egg at a time, thoroughly beating it in. Shape into round or oblong forms on an ungreased baking sheet, using 1 Tbsp. of the mixture for each one.

Bake at 450 degrees for 20 minutes. Reduce oven heat to 350 degrees and bake 20 minutes longer. Remove puffs from baking sheet; cool. When completely cooled, slit one side and fill with whipped cream or creamed filling.

Creamed filling: In the top of a double boiler, mix the flour, sugar, and salt. Stir in well-beaten eggs. Add scalded whole milk and blend thoroughly. Cook over boiling water, stirring constantly, for 4–5 minutes. Do *not* allow mixture to stick to bottom. Continue to cook at a medium heat for another 5 minutes, stirring less often. Cool in refrigerator. When chilled, add vanilla and fold in whipped cream.

Watermelon is tasty with salt.

Blessed is every one that feareth the Lord; that walketh in his ways. For thou shalt eat the labour of thine hands: happy shalt thou be, and it shall be well with thee. Thy wife shall be as a fruitful vine by the sides of thine house: thy children like olive plants round about thy table. —PSALM 128:1–3

RHUBARB SAUCE

3 c. diced rhubarb
1½ c. sugar (raw is fine)
2 Tbsp. cornstarch

⅛ tsp. salt
Juice of 1 orange

Boil all ingredients together until mixture is thickened and rhubarb is cooked.

Note from Bev

Delicious over vanilla ice cream!

GRANDMA'S APPLE CRISPETT

1 qt. peeled and sliced apples
½ c. water
¾ c. sugar

¾ c. brown sugar
1 c. flour
5 Tbsp. butter

Place apples in shallow baking dish; pour water over apples. Mix together remaining ingredients to make crust; sprinkle over apples and water. Do not stir together. Bake at 350 degrees for 45 minutes. When cool, cut in squares and serve with ice cream or whipped cream.

The best mirror is an old friend.
—German Proverb

Many hands make light work.

MOTHER'S CHERRY COBBLER

2 c. sour cherries

1/2 c. honey

2 Tbsp. flour or tapioca

1/2 c. fruit juice (orange or apple)

1 c. flour

1 tsp. baking powder

1/4 tsp. salt

1 Tbsp. honey

2 Tbsp. butter

6 Tbsp. milk

Mix cherries, honey, flour or tapioca, and fruit juice together and let stand 5 minutes. Pour into deep 10×16 baking dish.

Mix flour, baking powder, salt, and honey. Cut in the butter with pastry blender or fork. Add milk and mix until a soft dough is formed. Shape dough with hands (dust mixture and hands with flour first) until it fits over the cherries. Make slits in the dough to permit steam to escape.

Bake at 375 degrees for 30 minutes. Serve plain or with whipped cream, whipped topping, or ice cream.

Note from Bev

My mother and her whole family often picked cherries ``on the halves'' at her grandfather's farm in Strasburg. But the ``cherry-seeding party,'' especially, was the most memorable. The red juice stained her fingers and nails, and ran down her elbows. (Lemon juice and soapy water removed the stains.) This cobbler recipe is one of my mother's outstanding desserts. It's sure to bring smiles and requests for seconds.

Coconut Squares

½ c. butter

1½ c. brown sugar, divided

1 c. flour

2 eggs, beaten

1 tsp. vanilla

2 Tbsp. flour

¼ tsp. salt

½ tsp. baking powder

1½ c. coconut flakes

1 c. walnuts, chopped

Cream together butter and ½ c. brown sugar. Add 1 c. flour and work into crumbs with hands. Bake in a very slow oven—250 degrees—for 10 minutes or until done.

Meanwhile, add remaining brown sugar and vanilla to beaten eggs. Sift 2 Tbsp. flour and blend with salt and baking powder. Mix dry ingredients with egg and sugar mixture. Blend in coconut flakes and chopped walnuts. When crust is finished baking, pour mixture over the top. Return pan to oven and continue baking for an additional 25 minutes.

Favor is deceitful, and beauty is vain: but a woman that feareth the Lord, she shall be praised. —PROVERBS 31:30

Chocolate-Covered Strawberries

Melt semisweet chocolate. Hold strawberry by the stem and dip in chocolate. After the bottom is set, the top (including the stem) may be dipped in melted white chocolate—or the entire strawberry may be dipped in white chocolate.

Decorate with little swirls or patterns by using the opposite color chocolate or white chocolate tinted with food coloring.

Note from Bev

Delicious and elegant.

APPLE BETTY

Apple Betty:

7 c. tart baking apples (approximately 9 apples), peeled, cored, sliced, and cut into small pieces

1/4 c. raw or granulated sugar

1 1/2 c. (packed) brown sugar

1 Tbsp. cinnamon

1/8 tsp. salt

5 Tbsp. butter

3 c. tiny bread cubes (3–4 pieces of white bread, cut in 1/8" slivers, then cut the opposite way)

1/4 c. lemon juice

1/4 c. boiling water

Icing:

1/2 c. butter, softened

2 tsp. vanilla

1 3/4 c. confectioners' sugar, sifted (measure before sifting)

1 tsp. milk

Apple Betty: Mix apple pieces with 1/4 c. sugar; set aside. Mix brown sugar, cinnamon, and salt; set aside. (Note: after mixing, spoon brown sugar mixture lightly into measuring cup to measure.)

In saucepan, melt butter; add bread cubes and mix well. Set aside 1 c. of the buttered bread cubes; spread remaining bread cubes in the bottom of a buttered glass 9×9 baking dish. Arrange 3 c. of the sugared apples on top of the bread cubes; sprinkle with 3/4 c. of the loosely spooned brown sugar mixture. Spread 1/2 c. of the remaining buttered bread cubes over the brown sugar mixture. Layer the rest of the apples over bread cubes; sprinkle with all but 1/2 c. of the loosely spooned brown sugar mixture. Mix remaining brown sugar mixture with the remaining bread cubes and place on the top.

Mix lemon juice and boiling water. With a large spoon, sprinkle over the whole top. Bake dessert at 350 degrees for 1 hour. After removing from oven, allow to cool for 10–15 minutes. Add icing while still warm but not hot.

Icing: Cream butter with vanilla. Gradually add the sifted confectioners' sugar, beating until fluffy after each addition. Add the milk, beating until fluffy. Place spoonfuls on warm (but not hot) apple betty, spreading gently with a smooth table knife. (A spoon tends to create a bit of suction and would bring up some of the crumbs into the icing quicker than a smooth knife.)

Note from Bev

Absolutely tasty served with milk or light cream.

APPLE CRISP

3 lbs. baking apples (a bit tart)	2 c. flour
1 Tbsp. (rounded) granulated sugar	3 c. brown sugar
	1 Tbsp. cinnamon
	1 c. butter, softened
$^2/_3$ c. water	$^1/_2$ c. chopped pecans

Peel and slice apples; arrange in a buttered 9×13 glass pan. Lightly sprinkle with sugar; top with water.

Mix flour, brown sugar, and cinnamon in a bowl. Cut in butter with a pastry knife. Sprinkle crumbs over apples; sprinkle chopped pecans over the top. Bake at 375 degrees for approximately 45 minutes or until browned and bubbly.

Note from Bev

Serve hot with vanilla ice cream and hot tea or coffee.

PEACH DELIGHT

5–6 fresh peaches	4 vanilla wafers

Pit and slice peaches. Put vanilla wafers in a paper bag and crush with rolling pin. Put crumbs on piece of waxed paper; roll peaches in crumbs till peaches are covered. Serve in dessert dishes with whipped cream.

NUT BARS

¾ lb. dates, chopped

1 c. nutmeats, chopped

¾ c. oats

¼ c. flour

1 tsp. baking powder

¼ tsp. salt

3 eggs, beaten

1 c. brown sugar

Granulated sugar

Mix together dates, nutmeats, oats, flour, baking powder, and salt. Add brown sugar to beaten eggs; stir into flour mixture. Pour into greased 9×11 baking dish. Bake at 350 degrees for 25–30 minutes. When cool, cut into bars. Roll in granulated sugar.

A little house well filled, a little field well tilled, and a little wife well willed, are great riches.
—Benjamin Franklin

Puddings and Custards

Mary Ruth volunteered quickly when Mamma asked for someone to take one of two batches of graham-cracker pudding over to the Peacheys' the Thursday following Elias's funeral. Glad for an excuse to clear her head in the chilly air, she headed across the cornfield to the neighbors', low in spirit and dressed in the black garb of a mourner. Spying Adah's younger sister driving into the lane, she hurried to deliver the pudding to Miriam, then returned to help Dorcas unhitch the horse from the carriage.

—from *The Sacrifice*

(Note: See GRAHAM CRACKER PUDDING on page 119.)

GRAHAM CRACKER PUDDING

1 14-oz. can sweetened condensed milk, chilled, plus
enough regular milk to total
3 c.

¾ tsp. vanilla

1 large box instant vanilla
pudding mix (or ¾ c. bulk
instant vanilla pudding mix)

3 Tbsp. butter

1 c. crushed graham crackers,
divided

2 c. heavy whipping cream,
divided

Strawberries or blueberries,
optional

Mix cold milk (including sweetened condensed milk) and vanilla together. Gradually add pudding mix, stirring continually for 2 minutes; put in refrigerator.

Melt butter in saucepan and add crushed graham crackers. Stir over medium heat until lightly browned. Remove from heat.

Beat 1 c. heavy whipping cream until peaks form; fold together with ½ c. browned graham cracker crumbs and cooled pudding mixture. Pour into a 2-qt. serving dish. Reserving 1 Tbsp. crumbs, sprinkle remaining browned graham cracker crumbs over the pudding mixture; refrigerate.

Before serving, beat the remaining 1 c. of whipping cream and spread over the chilled mixture, making peaks with the whipped cream. Sprinkle reserved crumbs over the top to decorate. Serve immediately if possible; refrigerate leftovers.

Optional: Serve with sweetened strawberries or blueberries.

Banana Pudding: Fold 2 sliced bananas into pudding mixture before pouring into serving dish.

*To make eggs beat more quickly, add
a tiny pinch of salt to the whites.*

BUTTERSCOTCH PUDDING

Crust:

1½ c. flour

¾ c. melted butter

⅔ c. pecans, chopped

Mix these ingredients and press into a 9×13 pan. Bake at 350 degrees for 20 minutes. Cool completely.

Second layer:

1 8-oz. package cream cheese, softened

1 c. powdered sugar

1½ c. whipped topping

Beat these ingredients until smooth; spread onto cooled crust.

Third layer:

1 large pkg. instant butterscotch pudding

3 c. milk

Beat until thick; pour over second layer.

Fourth layer:

Spread additional whipped topping (as much as you wish) over pudding layer. Sprinkle with chopped pecans. Let stand several hours in fridge before serving.

RICE PUDDING

4 c. milk

⅓ c. uncooked rice

(20-minute rice—converted, enriched long grain)

⅓ c. sugar

⅓ c. raisins

¼ tsp. salt

¼ tsp. nutmeg

¼ tsp. cinnamon

Preheat over to 275 degrees. Combine all ingredients, except raisins, in saucepan on top of stove and bring to boil over medium heat, stirring constantly with a wooden spoon to avoid sticking. Continue stirring at a full boil over medium heat for 5 minutes. Bake immediately in buttered 1-½ qt. baking dish at 275 degrees for 2-¼ hours. (Open oven door only once to stir well at 1-¼ hours, then bake 1 more hour.) Remove from oven and stir, adding raisins. Cover 30–45 minutes. Serve warm or cold. Pudding thickens as it cools. Store in refrigerator.

CHOCOLATE CREAM PUDDING

2 c. milk	3 Tbsp. cocoa
3 Tbsp. cornstarch	¼ tsp. salt
½ c. sugar	1 tsp. vanilla

Scald milk by placing in the top of a double boiler and heating until a skin is formed over top of milk. Remove skin. Mix cornstarch, sugar, cocoa, and salt in a bowl. Add a small amount of scalded milk to form smooth paste. Gradually add rest of milk and vanilla. Chill.

DATE PUDDING

Syrup:

3 c. brown sugar	5 Tbsp. butter
5 c. water	

Batter:

4 c. flour	2 c. milk
1 tsp. salt	4 c. dates, chopped
8 tsp. baking powder	4 c. walnuts, chopped
2 c. brown sugar	Whipped cream

Syrup: Combine sugar and water. Boil for 2 minutes and add butter. Pour into 2 greased 9×13 inch pans.

Batter: Combine flour, salt, and baking powder. Add sugar and milk; mix well. Fold in dates and walnuts. Pour over syrup in pans; bake at 350 degrees for 40 minutes. To serve, alternate layers of date pudding and whipped cream in a glass dish.

Note from Bev

Makes an attractive dish to serve at Christmastime or other special occasions. Delicious any other time, as well.

Not that we are sufficient of ourselves to think any thing as of ourselves; but our sufficiency is of God.

—2 CORINTHIANS 3:5

Baby Pearl Tapioca

2 c. milk

2 rounded Tbsp. pearl tapioca

1/3 c. sugar

1/8 tsp. salt (optional)

1 egg, beaten

Whipped cream or whipped
    topping

Put milk and tapioca in top of double boiler; cook until tapioca is clear. Add sugar and salt. Add a little hot mixture to egg and stir, then mix all together, cooking until slightly thick. Allow to set until cool. Fold in whipped cream or whipped topping to taste.

Grape Mush Dessert

4 c. water

2 c. pure (100%) grape juice

1 1/2 c. sugar

1 small box raspberry Jell-O

2/3 c. instant Clear Jel*

1 c. water

1/2 tsp. salt

Juice of 2 lemons

Heat first 4 ingredients; stir in Clear Jel, 1 c. water, and salt. Mix in lemon juice. Chill. This makes a large amount!

*Instant Clear Jel can be purchased where canning supplies are available. Tapioca can be substituted if necessary.

Note from Bev

Delicious over Baby Pearl Tapioca.

EGG CUSTARD

4 c. milk	3 Tbsp. sugar
4 or 5 eggs	1 tsp. vanilla

Mix all ingredients together in order given. Bake in lightly greased custard cups at 350 degrees for 15–20 minutes.

PINEAPPLE CUSTARD

Pastry for a single-crust pie	1 c. sugar
1 20-oz. can crushed pine-	2 Tbsp. cornstarch
apple, drained	15 large marshmallows,
1 c. water	halved

Bake pie shell for 10 minutes; let cool. Boil pineapple, water, sugar, and cornstarch together until thick; pour into pie shell. Top with cut marshmallows. Bake at 350 degrees for 15 minutes or until topping is light brown.

FROZEN CUSTARD

1½ c. sugar	1 Tbsp. vanilla
1 Tbsp. flour	1 small can evaporated milk,
⅓ tsp. salt	chilled and whipped stiff*
3 c. boiling water	Crushed fruit of choice
2 eggs, beaten	

Mix sugar, flour, and salt. Add water and boil for three minutes, stirring constantly. Pour mixture over eggs slowly to prevent curdling. Return to heat and cook 2 more minutes. Cool. Add vanilla and fold in whipped evaporated milk; stir in crushed fruit of choice. Place in the freezer. For a smoother texture, whip again after the custard has just begun to freeze.

*Use more or less evaporated milk depending on how thick you want the custard to be.

CRACKER PUDDING

2 eggs, separated
1/2 c. plus 3 Tbsp. sugar, divided
4 c. whole milk
1 c. finely ground cracker crumbs (my grandmother used Eagle Butter crackers, but I substitute Le Petit Beurre golden toasted butter biscuits)
1/2 c. shredded coconut (or flakes)
Pinch of salt
1 tsp. vanilla

Beat egg yolks and 1/2 cup sugar; set aside. Scald milk in top of double boiler, stirring slowly. Gradually add egg yolk mixture to scalded milk, stirring continually. Cook for one full minute; then add cracker crumbs, coconut, and salt. Keep stirring! Once cracker crumbs are soft and the entire mixture is thick, remove from heat and add vanilla. Pour the mixture into a buttered 9×13 baking dish.

Create meringue by beating 3 Tbsp. sugar into stiffly beaten egg whites; spread over top of cracker pudding. Bake at 350 degrees for 30–40 minutes or until meringue is golden brown. Makes 6–8 servings.

Note from Bev

This is a very old, as well as scrumptious, Pennsylvania Dutch recipe. It was commonly served at Plain gatherings in Lancaster County, including our Ranck family reunions. I discovered it recently in my aunt Gladys Buchwalter's recipe notebook from the 1930s, written in her own hand when she was nineteen. In the autumn of that year, she was hired by a Lancaster dentist and his wife—the Paul Herr family—to cook, as well as to care for their young children.

Old-Fashioned Bread Pudding

4 slices stale bread, buttered
    and cut into small cubes
4 c. whole milk
4 eggs

¼ c. sugar
Pinch of salt
1 Tbsp. vanilla or pinch of
    nutmeg

Place bread cubes in milk and soak until very soft. Heat mixture until almost boiling. Set aside.

Beat eggs until light. Add eggs to sugar, salt, and vanilla or nutmeg. Mix well; stir into bread and milk mixture. Pour into greased medium baking dish and set in a pan of water. Bake at 300 degrees for 45 minutes.

Optional: Add ½ cup raisins to milk-soaked bread cubes for variety.

Snow Pudding and Dressing

Pudding:

2 c. water
¾ c. sugar
2 Tbsp. cornstarch

1 egg white, beaten until
    frothy
1 tsp. vanilla

Dressing:

½ c. sugar
1 Tbsp. cornstarch
1 big c. milk or water

1 egg yolk, beaten
Vanilla

Pudding: Bring water to boil. Mix sugar and cornstarch together; stir into boiling water. Cook until thickened, stirring constantly. Remove from heat. Beat in egg white and vanilla; chill. Serve cold—the colder the better.

Dressing: Mix sugar and cornstarch with milk or water; bring to a boil and cook until thick, stirring continually. Remove from heat and let cool slightly; stir in beaten egg yolk and a touch of vanilla. Serve over chilled pudding.

Cakes and Frostings

Lydia and Anna Mae got up to clear the table, bringing over an angel food cake for dessert. "Anna Mae baked this just for you, Aunt Sarah," Lydia said.

Anna Mae stood at Sarah's side, close enough to touch. "I want you to have the first piece." The girl grinned, showing her gums slightly.

"How nice of you," Sarah said, holding her plate while Anna Mae cut into the spongy white dessert.

—from *The Redemption of Sarah Cain*

(Note: see GOLDEN ANGEL FOOD CAKE on page 129.)

The ear that heareth the reproof of life abideth among the wise. —PROVERBS 15:31

GOLDEN ANGEL FOOD CAKE

9 eggs, separated, room
  temperature
1 tsp. vanilla
1 c. sugar,* divided

1 c. flour* (measure before
  sifting)
1/2 rounded tsp. cream of
  tartar

In small mixing bowl, beat egg yolks until thick and lemon colored (5 minutes or more, depending on beater). Add vanilla. Mix on low until blended. Gradually add 1/2 c. sugar. Continue to mix on low until blended, then beat 5 minutes more on high. Sprinkle part of the flour over yolk mixture; fold in by hand. Continue until all flour is folded in. Set aside and cover so batter doesn't dry out.

Thoroughly wash and dry beaters. Then, in a large mixing bowl, beat egg whites with cream of tartar on high until soft peaks form. Gradually add remaining 1/2 c. sugar. Beat on high until stiff peaks form. Take some of the egg whites and fold into the yolk mixture to soften. Add yolk mixture to stiff egg whites; fold together.

Gently pour batter into ungreased 10" tube pan with removable sides. Bake on lowest oven rack at 350 degrees for 50–60 minutes. When done, top will spring back when gently touched near the center. Immediately turn upside down until completely cool.

*Raw sugar and unbleached flour work very well.

Optional: Serve with fruit such as strawberries, peaches, or blueberries and whipped cream or milk.

CRUMB CAKE WITH FRESH APPLESAUCE

½ c. flour

¼ c. brown sugar

⅔ c. butter, divided, softened

¼ c. sugar

1 egg

1 c. sour milk or yogurt

1 tsp. baking soda

1 tsp. baking powder

Pinch of salt

2 c. flour

1 tsp. cinnamon

Mix flour, brown sugar, and 2⅔ Tbsp. butter by hand until crumbly; set aside. Cream together remaining ½ c. butter and remaining ingredients except for cinnamon; pour into greased 9×9 cake pan. Sprinkle with crumb mixture and cinnamon. Bake at 350 degrees for approximately 30 minutes or until the cake rises. Serve warm with applesauce.

When there's room in the heart,
there's room in the house.

RAISIN CAKE

2 c. hot water

2 c. seedless raisins

3 c. flour

1 tsp. salt

1 tsp. cinnamon

1 tsp. cloves

2 Tbsp. lard

2 c. brown sugar

2 eggs, stirred a bit with fork

1 tsp. baking soda, dissolved
    in a little hot water

Bring water and raisins to a boil. Sift together flour, salt, cinnamon and cloves. In separate bowl, cream together lard and brown sugar. Add the hot water, raisins, and eggs; mix well. Stir in dry ingredients and baking soda. Pour batter into two greased 9-inch round cake pans and bake at 350 degrees for 30 minutes.

CREAM CAKE AND FILLING

Cake:

1 Tbsp. butter

1 egg

1 c. sugar

1 c. sweetened condensed milk

2 c. flour

2 heaping Tbsp. baking powder

Vanilla extract

Filling:

1 egg, beaten

¼ c. flour or cornstarch

1 c. milk plus a little extra

½ tsp. vanilla

Cake: Cream together the butter and egg. Gradually add the sugar, sweetened condensed milk, flour, baking powder, and vanilla to taste. Pour into two greased 8-inch layer pans. Bake at 350 degrees for 35–40 minutes. Cool. Spread filling between layers and on top of cake.

Filling: Stir flour or cornstarch together with beaten egg; moisten with a little milk. Bring 1 c. milk to boil; stir in flour and egg mixture until thick. Flavor with vanilla.

SHOOFLY CAKE

4 c. flour

1 c. oil

1 lb. brown sugar

2 c. boiling water

1 c. molasses

2 tsp. baking soda

Mix together flour, oil, and brown sugar; work into crumbs. Reserve ½ c. of crumbs for topping. Stir remaining crumbs together with water, molasses, and baking soda until mixture is very thin. Pour into greased and floured 8×12 pan. Top with reserved crumbs and bake at 350 degrees for 45 minutes or until nice and brown.

Note from Bev

My family loves this cake. It is reminiscent of shoofly pie but is a completely different taste experience!

Mayonnaise Cake

1 c. boiling water

1 c. chopped nuts

2 tsp. baking soda

1 c. sugar

1 c. mayonnaise

2 c. flour

1 tsp. vanilla

1/2 c. brown sugar

1/2 c. nuts, chopped

1 c. chocolate chips

Combine first seven ingredients and mix well. Put in a greased and floured 9×13 pan. Combine brown sugar, nuts, and chocolate chips; sprinkle over batter. Bake at 300 degrees for 45 minutes.

Gingerbread

2 Tbsp. molasses

2 Tbsp. melted butter

1 c. sugar

1 tsp. cinnamon

1/2 tsp. cloves

1/4 tsp. ginger

1 tsp. salt

1 egg, well beaten

1 c. sour milk

1 tsp. baking soda

2 c. flour

Cream together molasses, butter, and sugar. Add spices and salt; mix well. Add egg, sour milk, baking soda, and flour, stirring slowly. Pour into a greased 8×8 pan. Bake at 350 degrees for 40 minutes.

Grandma's Gingerbread

1/4 c. butter

1/4 c. lard

1/2 c. sugar

1 c. hot water

1 egg

1 c. molasses

2 1/2 c. flour

1 1/2 tsp. baking soda

1 tsp. ginger

1 tsp. cinnamon

1/2 tsp. cloves

1/2 tsp. salt

Cream together butter, lard, and sugar. Add hot water to creamed mixture; beat smooth. Add remaining ingredients; beat until smooth. Bake in greased shallow pan at 325–350 degrees for 35 minutes.

*Serve applesauce on warm
gingerbread instead of
whipped cream.*

HOT WATER SPONGE CAKE

4 eggs, separated

2 c. sugar, divided

1 c. hot water

1 tsp. lemon juice

1 tsp. vanilla extract

2½ c. sifted flour (measure
after sifting)

1½ tsp. baking powder

½ tsp. salt

Beat egg whites by hand until stiff but not dry. Slowly stir in ¼ c. sugar. In separate bowl, beat egg yolks until light to lemon colored. Slowly add hot water and beat until mixture fills a large bowl. Gradually add in remaining sugar, then lemon juice and vanilla extract. Sift together dry ingredients; stir into egg yolk mixture. Gently fold in the egg whites. Pour into an ungreased tube cake pan. Start in cold oven and bake at 350 degrees for approximately 1 hour or until lightly browned.

SPICE CAKE

1 egg

3 egg yolks

2 c. brown sugar

½ c. butter, softened

½ c. milk

2 c. flour

1 tsp. baking soda

2 tsp. cream of tartar

2 tsp. cinnamon

½ tsp. cloves

1 tsp. nutmeg

Beat egg and egg yolks. Cream together brown sugar, butter, and milk; stir in beaten eggs. Mix dry ingredients together and blend well with creamed mixture. Pour batter into a greased tube or Bundt cake pan. Bake at 375 degrees for 30–40 minutes or until done.

Chocolate Cake

1 c. brown sugar

1 c. granulated sugar

1/2 c. butter, softened

4 eggs, separated

1/2 c. baking cocoa, dissolved
  in 1/2 c. boiling water

1 c. buttermilk

2 1/2 c. sifted flour

1 tsp. cream of tartar

1 tsp. baking soda

Big pinch of salt

1 tsp. vanilla

Cream together the sugars and butter for 15 minutes, beating by hand. Beat egg yolks; stir into creamed mixture. Mix in cocoa, buttermilk, and dry ingredients; add vanilla. Fold in beaten egg whites. Bake in greased pans at 375 degrees for 35 minutes or until done. Makes 2 large or 3 medium layers.

Note from Bev

Ideal with Butter Icing (see recipe on page 137).

White Chocolate Cake

Cake:

3/4 c. chopped or grated white
  chocolate

1/2 c. hot water

2 1/2 c. flour

1/2 tsp. baking powder

1/2 tsp. baking soda

1/2 tsp. salt

1 c. butter, softened

1 1/2 c. sugar

3 eggs, separated

1 c. buttermilk

1/2 c. chopped nuts

1/2 c. grated coconut

1 tsp. vanilla

Icing:

1/2 c. butter, softened

1 lb. confectioners' sugar

Pinch of salt

1 tsp. vanilla

3 Tbsp. milk (use more or less
  for desired consistency)

2 Tbsp. flour

Chopped nuts

Cake: In a small saucepan, melt white chocolate in hot water; set aside to cool. Sift together flour, baking powder, baking soda, and salt; set aside. Cream butter; add sugar and egg yolks. Cream well.

Slowly stir in white chocolate. Add dry ingredients alternately with buttermilk. Fold in nuts and coconut. Beat egg whites until they stand in peaks; add vanilla. Fold gently into batter. Line three 8-inch cake pans with wax paper. Pour batter into prepared pans and bake at 350 degrees for 30–35 minutes. Cool on wire racks.

Icing: Combine all ingredients except for nuts; beat well with electric mixer. Spread icing between cake layers and on top and sides; sprinkle with chopped nuts.

Gossip seems to travel faster over grapevines that are a slight bit sour.

GUMDROP CAKE

2 c. brown sugar	1 tsp. cinnamon
2 c. hot water	Peel and pulp from 1/4 orange,
1/2 c. shortening	ground
1 1/2 c. golden raisins	Peel and pulp from 1/2 lemon,
1/2 tsp. salt	ground
2 eggs, beaten	Juice from 1/2 lemon

Boil above ingredients together for 5 minutes; cool.

Mix together in a separate bowl:

1/2 tsp. baking soda, dissolved in 1 Tbsp. hot water	3/4 lb. pitted dates, cut in pieces with scissors
3 1/2 c. flour	1 c. pecans, chopped and browned in butter
1 lb. gumdrops (no black gumdrops)	

Stir both mixtures together. Pour into greased loaf pans, filling each half full. Bake at 250 degrees for 2–3 hours. Let cool before serving.

Pineapple Upside-Down Cake

Canned sliced pineapple

3 Tbsp. melted butter

1/2 c. brown sugar

1/3 c. shortening

1/2 c. sugar

1 egg

1 tsp. vanilla

1 1/4 c. flour

2 tsp. baking powder

1/4 tsp. salt

1/2 c. pineapple juice

Press pineapple slices between paper towels. Line the bottom of a greased 9-inch square cake pan with slightly moist pineapple slices. Cream together melted butter and brown sugar; pour over pineapple to make syrup. Mix together remaining ingredients; pour resulting batter gently over pineapple slices and syrup. Bake at 350 degrees for 30–35 minutes.

Be not overcome of evil, but overcome evil with good.

–ROMANS 12:21

Oatmeal Cake

Cake:

1 1/2 c. boiling water

1 c. unflavored instant
oatmeal

1 c. brown sugar

1 c. sugar

1/2 c. oil

2 eggs

1 1/2 c. flour

1 tsp. cinnamon

1 tsp. baking soda

1 tsp. salt (or a bit less)

Frosting:

1/2 c. butter

1 c. brown sugar

1/2 c. sweetened condensed
milk

1 tsp. vanilla

1 c. angel flake coconut

Cake: Pour boiling water over oatmeal; let stand to cool. Cream together sugars, oil, and eggs. Sift together dry ingredients; add to creamed mixture and blend well. Add oatmeal and mix again. Pour batter into greased and floured loaf pan. Bake for 35–40 minutes at 350 degrees.

Frosting: Melt together butter, brown sugar, and sweetened condensed milk in a small saucepan. Cook, stirring constantly, until thick; remove from heat. Add vanilla and coconut; stir until well mixed. Spread over cake.

Watch and pray, that ye enter not into temptation: the spirit indeed is willing, but the flesh is weak.   —MATTHEW 26:41

MIDNIGHT CAKE

1½ c. sugar	2 eggs
¼ c. butter, softened	1 tsp. vanilla
¼ c. lard	2 c. flour
½ c. baking cocoa	1 tsp. baking soda
⅛ tsp. salt	1 c. buttermilk

Cream together sugar, butter, and lard. Mix in cocoa and salt. Add eggs and vanilla; beat well for 3 minutes. Gradually mix in flour and baking soda, then buttermilk. Beat well for 5 minutes. Pour into two 8-inch round greased and floured pans. Bake at 350 degrees for 30–35 minutes or until toothpick inserted near center comes out clean. Cool. Frost with CHOCOLATE PEANUT BUTTER FROSTING (page 138).

BUTTER ICING

¼ c. butter, melted	Whole milk (enough to make
2 c. confectioners' sugar	a heavy paste when blend-
3 drops vanilla extract	ing with butter and sugar)

Beat all ingredients together well and spread on cake.

CHOCOLATE PEANUT BUTTER FROSTING

3 heaping Tbsp. creamy
   peanut butter
3 heaping Tbsp. soft butter
1 tsp. vanilla

2 c. powdered sugar
3 heaping Tbsp. cocoa
1/8 tsp. salt
2–4 Tbsp. milk

Mix together peanut butter, butter, and vanilla. Stir in sugar, cocoa, and salt. Add milk, stirring, until desired consistency is reached.

Note from Bev

Really terrific on Midnight Cake. Ideal frosting for a two-layer cake.

COCOA FLUFF ICING

6 Tbsp. butter, softened
1 1/2 tsp. vanilla
1/2 c. baking cocoa

1/2 c. milk*
3 c. confectioners' sugar

Cream the butter; stir in vanilla and cocoa. Add the milk and confectioners' sugar alternately, beating until light and fluffy after each addition. Spread on cake, making swirls with the tip of a smooth table knife.

*Use less milk if necessary; icing should be thick enough to hold its form.

Pies

Especially now, at summer's onset, when strawberries are ripe and ready for pies and preserves, I think of Jonas. He loved strawberry-rhubarb pie like nobody's business, and both his mamma and mine made it for him with sugar and raw honey, so it was nothing short of wonderful-good. "Desserts are s'posed to be plenty sweet," Mamma has said for as long as I can remember. This, with her irresistible wide-eyed smile. These days Sadie is the one baking such delicious fruit pies for Jonas.

—from *The Sacrifice*

(Note: See STRAWBERRY-RHUBARB PIE on page 143.)

PIE CRUST

3 c. flour

2 c. shortening

¼ c. sugar

½ c. water

Pinch of salt

Mix ingredients together until they form a soft ball. Use plenty of flour when rolling out dough. Makes 1 double crust or 2 single crusts.

Note: Placing the dough on a piece of wax paper makes it easier to put in the pie tin.

"New Mercies"

After the sowing of springtime,
After the showers of rain,
Cometh the blossoms of summer,
Cometh the fruit and the grain.

After the summer comes autumn
And harvest of seed early sown;
After the richness of autumn
A welcome of winter's white gown!

Just so our lives know unfolding:
After each turn of our way
Always a blessed revealing
Of God's new purpose each day.

New ev'ry morning His mercies,
Never an end to His care;
After our pilgrimage journey,
Fullness of glory to share.
—Alice Reynolds Flower

PIE DOUGH

4 c. flour
1½ tsp. salt
1 Tbsp. sugar
1½ c. shortening

1 egg
½ c. cold water
1 Tbsp. vinegar

Mix flour, salt, sugar, and shortening together to form crumbs. Beat egg, water, and vinegar; add to crumbs and stir with fork until mixture forms a ball. Roll crusts out and place in pans. Makes 5–6 single crusts.

Note from Bev

This recipe makes quite a few crusts, but they store nicely in the freezer for quick use later.

LEMON SPONGE PIE

3 eggs, separated
2 c. sugar
5 Tbsp. lemon juice
3 Tbsp. melted butter

¼ c. flour
2 c. warm milk
9-inch unbaked pie crust

Beat egg yolks. Add sugar, lemon juice, and melted butter; mix well. Stir in flour and milk.

In separate bowl, beat egg whites until they form stiff peaks; fold into the first mixture. Pour into unbaked pie crust and bake at 425 degrees for 10 minutes. Reduce heat to 325 degrees and continue baking for 35 minutes.

Note from Bev

One of my all-time favorite Amish pies!

Spread butter or margarine on both sides of knife when cutting a meringue pie.

STRAWBERRY-RHUBARB PIE

1½ c. diced rhubarb
½ c. water
½ c. raw honey
½ c. sugar

1 3-oz. pkg. strawberry Jell-O
1 generous c. vanilla ice cream
Pre-baked pie shell for 9-inch
  pie

Cook rhubarb in water until tender; sweeten with honey and sugar. Cool; puree in blender.

Prepare Jell-O as directed on package and chill until almost set. Remove from refrigerator and add pureed rhubarb and vanilla ice cream. Beat thoroughly. Place mixture in pre-baked pie shell and refrigerate until firm. Makes one 9-inch pie.

Optional: Slice a few fresh strawberries on top. Also, strawberry ice cream can be used instead of vanilla ice cream.

Note from Bev

One of my mother's well-loved pie recipes. She often makes this without the rhubarb and serves it with or without a pie crust. It is delightful and refreshing either way!

SNITZ PIE

3 gallons apple butter
3 gallons applesauce
5 c. sugar
½ c. lemon juice
1 rounded Tbsp. cinnamon
1 rounded Tbsp. cloves

½ c. butter, melted
1 c. Clear Jel* or minute
  tapioca
1 tsp. salt
Pastry for 20–24 double-crust
  pies

Stir all ingredients together and fill unbaked pie shells; top with crust. Bake pies at 350 degrees for 1 hour or until done. Makes 20–24 pies.

*Clear Jel is available where canning supplies are sold.

INDIANA SHOOFLY PIE

1 c. flour

$^2/_3$ c. brown sugar

1 rounded Tbsp. shortening or margarine

1 c. molasses

$^3/_4$ c. hot water

1 egg

1 tsp. baking soda dissolved in $^1/_4$ cup hot water

Pastry for 9-inch single-crust pie

Combine flour, brown sugar, and shortening; make crumbs either by hand or using a pastry blender. Set aside $^1/_2$ c. crumbs to put on top of finished pie.

Combine molasses, hot water, egg, and baking soda dissolved in water; mix well. Stir crumbs into liquid. Pour resulting mixture into pie crust and top with reserved crumbs. Bake at 375 degrees for 35 minutes.

Note from Bev

Delicious served slightly warm with ice cream or whipped cream. This makes an excellent pie and won first prize many times at farm show judging. It was also a popular choice at Mary Jane Hoober's family restaurant for many years.

LANCASTER COUNTY WET-BOTTOM SHOOFLY PIE

Syrup Mixture:

2 large eggs

$2^2/_3$ c. Ole Barrel syrup*

$1^1/_2$ tsp. baking soda

2 c. boiling water

In a small mixing bowl, beat eggs with electric mixer until thick. Beat in syrup. Stir in baking soda. Gradually add boiling water, stirring continually until mixed. Set aside until completely cool. If in a hurry, set bowl in cold water and stir gently until cool.

*Ole Barrel syrup will produce the best results. However, if it is unavailable in your area, a thick corn syrup may be substituted.

Crumbs:

2¹/₂ c. flour	¹/₈ tsp. salt
1¹/₂ c. brown sugar	2 Tbsp. shortening

Pastry for two 9.5-inch single-crust pies

In a large bowl, mix together flour, brown sugar, and salt. Cut shortening into flour mixture with a pastry blender. Set 1¹/₃ c. crumb mixture aside in a small bowl. Pour approximately 1 c. syrup mixture into remaining crumb mixture; mix by hand to make a thick, smooth paste. Add remaining syrup mixture approximately 1 c. at a time, stirring well after each addition to keep mixture as smooth as possible.

Pour syrup and crumb mixture into pie crusts; sprinkle half of reserved crumbs evenly on each pie. Bake at 375 degrees for 10 minutes; reduce heat to 350 degrees and bake for 30 more minutes. If center of pie is not set at the end of this time, turn oven off and leave pies in the oven for 5–15 minutes more. Delicious served hot with vanilla ice cream. Shoofly pie seems even better the day after it is made.

Note from Bev

There are many recipes for shoofly pie. However, the best pies are those with a gooey or wet bottom. I distinctly remember eating this delicious pie at church and family gatherings in Lancaster County. There's really nothing to compare with this sweet offering. Makes my mouth water just remembering. . . .

Blessed are the meek: for they shall inherit the earth.

—MATTHEW 5:5

PEANUT BUTTER PIE

8 oz. cream cheese, softened

12 oz. confectioners' sugar
(approximately 1½ c.)

7½ oz. creamy peanut butter

1 c. whole milk

16 oz. whipped cream

2 graham cracker pie crusts,
baked

Beat the cream cheese on low speed until soft and fluffy. Stir in sugar and peanut butter. Slowly add milk, beating constantly. Fold in whipped cream. Pour mixture into graham cracker pie crusts; freeze until firm, about 4 hours.

Note from Bev

A chocolate pie crust with a sprinkling of walnuts is also an option. So tasty!

PUMPKIN CHIFFON PIE

1 envelope unflavored gelatin

¼ c. cold water

3 eggs, separated

1 c. sugar, divided

1¼ c. canned pumpkin

½ c. milk

½ tsp. salt

½ tsp. ginger

½ tsp. nutmeg

½ tsp. cinnamon

Pastry for single-crust pie,
baked

Soften gelatin in cold water; set aside. Beat egg yolks slightly; add ½ c. sugar, pumpkin, milk, salt, and spices. Cook in double boiler until thick. Add softened gelatin to hot pumpkin mixture; mix thoroughly and cool. Beat egg whites until stiff; stir in remaining sugar. When pumpkin mixture begins to thicken, fold in egg whites. Pour into baked pie shell; chill in refrigerator.

Note: Pie may be garnished with whipped cream before serving.

APPLE MINCEMEAT PIE

2 c. apples, coarsely ground	2 c. sugar
³/₄ c. raisins	Water
½ lb. lean ground beef, browned	Pastry for two 9-inch double-crust pies
½ tsp. cloves	2 Tbsp. vinegar

In saucepan, blend together apples, raisins, browned ground beef, cloves, and sugar. Add a little water and bring to a boil; place mixture into pie shells. Sprinkle 1 Tbsp. vinegar on each pie before covering with top crust. Bake pies at 350 degrees for 50–60 minutes. Serve warm with vanilla ice cream.

A fresh egg will sink to the bottom on its side in a deep pan of water. If it is not good, it will stand on end or float.

BLUEBERRY PIE

2 c. sour cream	1 unbaked graham cracker pie crust
1 c. sugar	
¼ c. sifted flour	2 c. canned, ready-to-use blueberry pie filling
½ tsp. salt	
³/₄ tsp. almond extract	½ c. whipped cream
2 eggs	

Combine first six ingredients; beat well and pour into pie crust. Bake at 375 degrees for 25 minutes. Remove from oven and spread with blueberry pie filling. Cool and refrigerate. When chilled, spread whipped cream on top.

Rich Chocolate Pie

Cream ½ c. butter with ¾ c. sugar. Stir in 2 squares of unsweetened baking chocolate, melted and cooled. Add 2 eggs, one at a time, beating for 5 minutes on high speed after each addition. Fold in 2 c. whipped cream. Pour into baked 9-inch pie crust. Chill until firm, about 2 hours. Can be frozen, as well.

Note from Bev

A very rich pie, but so luscious. It makes 12 small portions. Enjoy!

Pumpkin Torte

2½ c. graham cracker crumbs	3 egg yolks
⅓ c. sugar	½ c. sugar
½ c. butter, softened	½ c. milk
2 eggs, beaten	½ tsp. salt
¾ c. sugar	1 Tbsp. cinnamon
8 oz. cream cheese, softened	3 egg whites
1 envelope gelatin	¼ c. sugar
¼ c. cold water	1 c. whipped cream
2 c. pumpkin (cooked or canned)	

Mix together graham cracker crumbs, ⅓ c. sugar, and butter; press into 9×13 baking pan. Mix together beaten eggs, ¾ c. sugar, and cream cheese; pour over graham cracker crust. Bake at 350 degrees for 20 minutes. Cool.

Dissolve gelatin in cold water. Cook pumpkin, egg yolks, ½ c. sugar, milk, salt, and cinnamon until mixture thickens. Remove from heat and add dissolved gelatin; cool.

Beat egg whites and ¼ c. sugar together; fold into pumpkin mixture. Pour over cooled, baked crust. Top with whipped cream.

Vanilla Pie

Bottom part:

½ c. brown sugar	1 egg
½ c. molasses	1 c. water
1 Tbsp. flour	1 tsp. vanilla

9-inch unbaked pie crust

Top part:

1 c. flour	½ tsp. soda
½ c. brown sugar	½ tsp. baking powder
¼ c. butter-flavored shorten-ing	

In saucepan, combine ingredients for bottom part of pie, except the vanilla, and cook till thickened. Allow to cool; stir in vanilla. Pour into unbaked pie crust. In separate bowl, combine ingredients for top part, mixing until crumbly. Spread over bottom layer of pie. Bake at 350 degrees for 40–45 minutes. (Depending on the oven, pie might be done in only 30 minutes.)

Pecan Pie

3 eggs	1 c. dark corn syrup
½ c. sugar	1 c. broken pecans
½ tsp. salt	Pastry for 9-inch pie
⅓ c. melted butter	

Beat eggs, sugar, salt, melted butter, and corn syrup until well mixed. Add pecans and pour into a 9-inch pastry-lined pie pan. Bake at 350 degrees for 40–50 minutes.

Note from Bev

I can't recall a single Christmas dinner while I was growing up that did not include this fantastic pie. Pecan pie, to my mind, equals the warm and fond memory of family, friends, and delightful fellowship.

WEEPLESS PIE MERINGUE

1 Tbsp. cornstarch	2 egg whites
2 tsp. water	2 Tbsp. sugar
½ c. boiling water	

Moisten cornstarch with 2 tsp. water. Stir in boiling water; cook over low heat until thick, stirring constantly. Set aside to cool. Beat egg whites and sugar until slightly stiff. Gradually beat in cooled cornstarch mixture until it forms peaks. Pile meringue on pie; brown.

Note from Bev

``Weepless´´ means this meringue never fails.

When ye come together to eat, tarry one for another.

—I CORINTHIANS 11:33

Cookies and Candies

Together, she and Lizzie had made a big batch of peanut-butter balls dipped in melted chocolate, several dozen sand tarts, candied dates, and crystal stick candy at Lizzie's house yesterday. They'd had a laughing good time doing so. The best part of all was there were still plenty of sweets to go around, even having shared a considerable portion with Cousin Peter and Fannie's wee ones.

—from *The Sacrifice*

(Note: see SAND TARTS, PEANUT BUTTER BALLS, CRYSTAL STICKS, and CANDIED DATES on pages 158, 167, 169, and 170.)

BUTTERSCOTCH ICEBOX COOKIES

1½ c. melted shortening

1 c. brown sugar

1 c. sugar

3 eggs, well beaten

1 c. chopped nuts

1 tsp. salt

4½ c. flour

2 tsp. baking soda

1 tsp. cinnamon

½ tsp. nutmeg

½ tsp. cloves

Cream melted shortening with sugars. Gradually stir in eggs, then mix in nuts. Sift dry ingredients together and add to creamed mixture; mix well. Shape into a 2½-inch-thick roll. Wrap in waxed paper and refrigerate overnight or until firm. Slice cookie dough into ⅛-inch slices with sharp knife.

Preheat oven to 425 degrees. Bake on ungreased cookie sheets for 5 to 6 minutes. Makes 75 cookies.

PINEAPPLE COOKIES

½ c. shortening

½ c. brown sugar

½ c. sugar

1 egg

2 c. sifted flour

1 tsp. baking powder

½ tsp. salt

1 c. crushed pineapple

½ c. chopped walnuts

Cream shortening and sugars. Add egg; beat thoroughly. Sift together dry ingredients; add to creamed mixture alternately with pineapple. Stir in nuts. Drop by teaspoonfuls on greased cookie sheets, allowing 4 inches between each cookie.

Bake at 350 degrees for 15–18 minutes. Makes about 3½ dozen cookies.

And it was in my mouth as honey for sweetness.

–EZEKIEL 3:3

DROPPED AMISH CHURCH SUGAR COOKIES

3½ c. flour

1 tsp. baking powder

1 tsp. baking soda

1 tsp. ground nutmeg

1 tsp. salt

1½ c. margarine (no substitutes)

2 c. white sugar

1 tsp. vanilla extract

1 tsp. almond extract

2 eggs, slightly beaten

1 c. sour cream

Sugar

Preheat oven to 375 degrees. Stir together flour, baking powder, baking soda, nutmeg, and salt. In large bowl, beat margarine, sugar, and extracts until creamy. Add eggs and sour cream; beat well. Gradually add dry ingredients, mixing well.

Grease cookie sheets or line them with parchment paper. Using medium-sized cookie scoop, drop cookies 2 inches apart. Sprinkle with sugar.

Bake cookies for 10–15 minutes or until set. Don't allow cookies to get too golden. Remove from cookie sheet and place on cooling rack. When completely cool, store between sheets of waxed paper.

Note from Bev

The perfect cookie for holiday gatherings of any kind . . . and for all ages, from Indiana Amish country!

OLD-FASHIONED WALNUT OR PECAN DROPS

4 egg whites, room temperature (approx. ⅔ c.)

3½ c. powdered sugar (measure before sifting)

1 lb. black walnuts or pecans, finely chopped

2 Tbsp. flour, sifted (measure before sifting)

Beat the egg whites until very light and soft peaks form. Sprinkle some of the sifted powdered sugar over the beaten egg whites; beat in. Repeat until all the powdered sugar is mixed in and the mixture is very light; then add nuts and sifted flour. Mix gently.

Drop by half spoonfuls onto buttered cookie sheets. (Drops should be about the size of a silver dollar.) Bake at 325 degrees for 20 minutes. Serve cool.

HERMITS

1½ c. granulated or brown
    sugar
1 c. shortening or butter
2½ c. flour
3 eggs
1 tsp. cinnamon

1 tsp. baking soda, dissolved
    in 2 Tbsp. boiling water
1 lb. English walnuts, chopped
¾ c. chopped raisins, boiled
    until soft

Mix together all ingredients except walnuts and raisins. Drain off the water from raisins; add both raisins and walnuts to mixture and blend thoroughly. Drop by teaspoon onto greased cookie sheet, about 1½ inches apart. Bake at 325 degrees for 15 minutes or until lightly browned.

Note from Bev

A very old recipe from Grandmother Ada, as well as her mother's recipe files. This cookie is quite popular in Amish country.

CHOCOLATE CHEER-UP COOKIES

½ c. butter
1 egg
⅓ c. sugar
½ c. brown sugar
½ tsp. vanilla
1 c. sifted flour

½ tsp. salt
½ tsp. baking soda
1½ oz. semisweet chocolate,
    melted
½ c. M&M's

Cream together butter, egg, sugars, and vanilla. Sift together dry ingredients; combine with creamed mixture. Stir in melted chocolate and M&M's. Drop on greased cookie sheets and bake at 375 degrees for 12–14 minutes or until brown.

Note from Bev

The perfect encouragement gift for a shut-in or sad friend. This is my daughter Julie's original recipe. Delicious!

The fear of the Lord is the instruction of wisdom; and before honour is humility. —PROVERBS 15:33

CHOCOLATE CHRISTMAS COOKIES

Cookies:

4 c. flour

1 tsp. baking soda

½ tsp. salt

1 c. butter, softened

2 c. light brown sugar

2 eggs

2 tsp. instant coffee granules

¾ c. baking cocoa

¼ c. olive oil

1⅓ c. sour cream

2 c. angel flake coconut

2 c. English walnuts, chopped

Icing:

6 Tbsp. baking cocoa

2 Tbsp. olive oil

½ c. sour cream

½ c. butter, softened

4 c. confectioners' sugar

Cookies: Mix together flour, baking soda, and salt; set aside. Beat together butter, sugar, eggs, coffee, cocoa, olive oil, and sour cream. Gradually stir in the dry ingredients. Add coconut and walnuts; mix well. Drop by tablespoons onto greased baking sheets; bake at 350 degrees for 10 minutes. Spread with the following icing when completely cool.

Icing: Mix together cocoa, olive oil, sour cream, and butter. Stir in confectioner's sugar until desired consistency is reached.

Baking powder removes tea and coffee stains from cups and porcelain pots.

"My Christmas Wish for You"

This year at blessed Christmastide,
My dearest wish for you
Comes wrapped in love and peace and joy,
God's precious gift to make us new.
Courage in the midst of fear.
Joy in the midst of sorrow,
Healing for pain,
Hope for tomorrow.
This Christmas wish I offer you,
Came as Mary's babe, God's only Son.
This blessed gift so dear, so true—
For you and everyone.
—Beverly Lewis

PUMPKIN COOKIES

1/2 c. shortening	1/2 c. raisins
1 c. sugar	1 tsp. salt
1 egg	1/2 tsp. baking soda
1 3/4 c. flour	1/2 tsp. baking powder
1 c. pumpkin	1 tsp. cinnamon
1 c. All-Bran cereal	1/2 tsp. ground cloves
1/2 c. chopped nuts	1/4 tsp. nutmeg

Mix together shortening, sugar, and egg. Stir in remaining ingredients until well blended. Drop onto lightly greased cookie sheet; bake at 375 degrees for 7–10 minutes.

Note from Bev

The lovely smell of these cookies, freshly baked, brings back happy memories of returning home from school and finding Mother waiting, all smiles.

Take heed that ye do not your alms before men, to be seen of them: otherwise ye have no reward of your Father which is in heaven.
                                                                        —MATTHEW 6:1

SAND TARTS

½ c. butter, softened	1 tsp. baking powder
1 c. sugar	1½ c. flour
1 Tbsp. whole milk	Blanched almonds, halved
1 tsp. vanilla	¼ tsp. cinnamon
2 eggs, separated	2 Tbsp. sugar
½ tsp. salt	

Cream butter and sugar; stir in whole milk, vanilla, and egg yolks. Mix until well blended and light. Sift together salt, baking powder, and flour; stir into creamed mixture and mix well. Chill for 3 hours.

On lightly floured surface, roll dough out exceptionally thin. Cut out cookies, using 3-inch star or heart cookie cutters. Place cookies on greased cookie sheet with an almond half centered on each cookie. Beat egg whites into a glaze. Mix together cinnamon and sugar. Brush cookies lightly with beaten egg whites and sprinkle with cinnamon-sugar topping. Bake at 375 degrees for 8 minutes or until cookies are slightly brown on the edges. (They burn easily, so watch carefully). Makes 30 cookies.

Note from Bev

What a cookie—none are more delicate than this! My sister and I liked to help Mother bake them on Christmas Eve afternoon so we could nibble on them while we trimmed the tree with our parents that evening.

Carrot Cookies

Cookies:

1 c. shortening

³/₄ c. sugar

1 egg

2 c. flour

2 tsp. baking powder

¹/₂ tsp. salt

1 c. cooked, mashed carrots

1 tsp. vanilla

Frosting:

3 c. confectioners' sugar

Juice of 1 orange (approx.
¹/₄ c.)

1–2 Tbsp. grated orange rind

Cookies: Blend shortening, sugar, and egg. Sift together dry ingredients; stir into creamed mixture along with carrots and vanilla. Mix thoroughly; drop on cookie sheet. Bake at 375 degrees for 15 minutes. Makes 5 dozen.

Frosting: Mix confectioners' sugar into orange juice until very smooth and right consistency for frosting. Mix in grated orange rind. Spread on cooled cookies.

Note from Bev

Watch guests light up when they bite into these lovely cookies!

Zucchini Cookies

¹/₂ c. butter

¹/₂ c. honey

1 egg

¹/₂ tsp. vanilla

1 c. raw zucchini, skinned and grated

2 c. flour

1 tsp. cinnamon

1 tsp. cloves

1 tsp. baking soda

Nuts or raisins

Cream butter, honey, egg, and vanilla together. Stir in zucchini. Sift together dry ingredients; stir into creamed mixture. Stir in nuts or raisins. Bake as drop cookies on greased cookie sheets at 325 degrees for 12–15 minutes.

CRANBERRY CRUNCHIES

1 c. uncooked rolled oats

½ c. flour

1 c. brown sugar

½ c. butter or margarine

1-lb. can cranberry sauce (jel-
lied or whole)

Mix oats, flour, and brown sugar in a bowl. Cut in the butter with a dull knife until mixture is crumbly. Place half the mixture in an 8×8 greased baking dish; cover with all the cranberry sauce. Spread the rest of the crumb mixture over the top. Bake at 350 degrees for 45 minutes. Cut into squares and serve hot or cold topped with vanilla ice cream.

Therefore all things whatsoever ye would that men should do to you, do ye even so to them: for this is the law and the prophets. —MATTHEW 7:12 (The Golden Rule)

CHOCOLATE CHIP COOKIES

1 c. butter, softened

1 c. sugar

½ c. brown sugar, packed

1 tsp. vanilla

2 eggs

2¼ c. flour, sifted

1 tsp. baking soda

1 tsp. salt

12 oz. chocolate chips

1 c. chopped walnuts
(optional)

Cream together butter, sugars, and vanilla until light and fluffy. Beat in eggs. Sift together flour, baking soda, and salt; gradually add to creamed mixture, mixing until well blended. Fold in chocolate chips and walnuts. Drop on greased cookie sheets and bake at 375 degrees for about 10 minutes. Makes 5 dozen 3-inch cookies.

SUGARLESS COOKIES

1 c. raisins

½ c. chopped dates

½ c. chopped apples

½ c. water

½ c. shortening

2 eggs, beaten

1 Tbsp. honey

1 tsp. vanilla

1 tsp. soda

1 c. flour

½–¾ c. chopped nuts

Boil raisins, dates, and apples in ½ cup water for 3 minutes. Mix in shortening; cool. Add beaten eggs, honey, vanilla, and soda to mixture, then stir in flour and nuts. Refrigerate until chilled. Drop by teaspoons on well-greased cookie sheet; bake at 350 degrees for 10–12 minutes. Refrigerate in airtight containers.

Train up a child in the way he should go: and when he is old, he will not depart from it. —PROVERBS 22:6

ORANGE COOKIES

½ c. butter or margarine, softened

1 c. sugar, divided

¼ c. brown sugar

1 egg, beaten

1½ c. sifted flour

¼ tsp. cream of tartar

½ tsp. baking soda

2 Tbsp. whole milk

3 tsp. grated orange rind

8 tsp. orange juice

Cream together butter, ½ c. sugar, and brown sugar; add beaten egg and mix well. Sift together the dry ingredients; stir into creamed mixture along with milk and orange rind. Mix remaining sugar with orange juice; stir into dough. Bake as drop cookies on greased cookie sheets at 375 degrees for 10–15 minutes.

AUNT DOTTIE'S PEANUT BUTTER COOKIES

$^1/_2$ c. margarine, butter, or
  shortening

$^1/_2$ c. peanut butter

$^1/_2$ c. sugar

$^1/_2$ c. brown sugar

1 egg, beaten

$1^1/_4$ c. flour

$^1/_4$ tsp. salt

$^3/_4$ tsp. baking soda

$^1/_2$ tsp. baking powder

Cream together the margarine, peanut butter, and sugars. Add the beaten egg and mix all together. Sift dry ingredients and add to the mixture. Chill cookie dough. Roll into small balls and place on greased cookie sheets. Press with fork and bake at 375 degrees for 12–15 minutes. Makes about 4 dozen cookies.

SNICKERDOODLES

$^1/_2$ c. butter, softened

$^3/_4$ c. sugar

1 egg

$1^3/_8$ cups sifted flour

1 tsp. cream of tartar

$^1/_2$ tsp. soda

$^1/_4$ tsp. salt

2 Tbsp. sugar

2 tsp. cinnamon

Mix together butter, sugar, and egg. Sift together flour, cream of tartar, soda, and salt; stir into creamed mixture. Chill dough for 1 hour. Roll into balls the size of small walnuts. Combine sugar and cinnamon; roll balls in mixture. Place cookies 2–3 inches apart on ungreased baking sheets.

Bake at 400 degrees until lightly browned, approximately 6–8 minutes. (Cookies puff up at first, then flatten out with a crinkled top). Makes 3 dozen cookies.

Note from Bev

I'm so fond of these cookies I created a story line around them in one of my books for girls, No Guys Pact (HOLLY'S HEART series). My mother baked them often all the years I was growing up, and I enjoy making them now for my own family.

And be ye kind one to another, tenderhearted, forgiving one another.

—EPHESIANS 4:32

FILLED COOKIES

1/2 c. shortening	1 egg
1 c. sugar	1/4 c. milk
3/4 tsp. salt	3 c. flour
1 tsp. vanilla	1 Tbsp. baking powder

Combine all ingredients and mix, using slow speed on mixer. Roll dough out and cut into circles. Place a spoonful of desired filling on half of the cookies (see options). Moisten edges of cookies with water; top with remaining cookies. Prick the top cookies and press down around filling to seal. Place cookies on greased cookie sheets and bake at 375 degrees for 10 minutes or until browned.

Filling options: Mincemeat, fig filling, date and nut filling, dried apricots (boil in a bit of water until apricots are soft or desired consistency and sweeten to taste, using approximately 1 c. sugar per 1 c. fruit).

Oven-cleaning tip (for non-self-cleaning ovens): In a cool oven, place 2 c. of soapy water in a shallow porcelain baking pan along with 3 Tbsp. ammonia. Close the oven door and let set overnight. Because the ammonia fumes will dissolve much of the grease, it is possible to clean the oven with little effort.

GINGERSNAPS

1 c. sugar

1/3 c. molasses

1/2 c. butter or margarine

1 egg

1 tsp. ginger

1 tsp. cinnamon

1/2 tsp. cloves

2 c. flour

Pinch of salt

1 tsp. baking soda, dissolved
   in approximately 1/4 tsp.
   warm water

Sugar

Combine 1 c. sugar, molasses, butter, and egg in a bowl; mix well. Blend in all remaining ingredients except for remaining sugar. Chill dough. Roll into approximately 1-inch balls; roll in sugar. Place about 2 inches apart on lightly greased cookie sheets, as cookies tend to spread. Bake at 350 degrees for 7–9 minutes or until edges are firm.

BUTTERMILK COOKIES

1 c. margarine or butter,
   softened

2 c. sugar

3 eggs, beaten

1/2 tsp. salt

1 tsp. baking powder

1/2 tsp. nutmeg

4 1/2 c. flour

1 c. buttermilk

Cream butter and sugar together. Add beaten eggs to the creamed mixture. Combine dry ingredients in a separate bowl; add to creamed mixture alternately with the buttermilk. Drop dough onto a well-greased cookie sheet and bake at 350 degrees for about 15 minutes. For variety, add cooked raisins or nuts to dough.

Note from Bev

This recipe belonged to my paternal great-grandmother, Lettie Jones, mother of nine children and cookie-maker extraordinaire. Baked with her loving touch in each cookie.

Our Father God, thy name we praise
To thee our hymns addressing,
And joyfully our voices raise
Thy faithfulness confessing;
Assembled by thy grace, O Lord,
We seek fresh guidance from thy word.
Now grant anew thy blessing!
—from Songs of the Ausbund

DATE OR RAISIN COOKIES

2¼ c. dates or raisins,
  chopped
1 c. sugar
1 c. water
1 c. chopped walnuts
1 c. shortening

2 c. brown sugar
3 eggs
4 c. flour
½ tsp. salt
½ tsp. baking soda

In saucepan, mix chopped dates or raisins, sugar, and water. Boil slowly, stirring continually, for about 10 minutes. Remove from heat and add chopped walnuts; set aside to cool.

In large mixing bowl, cream together shortening and brown sugar. In a separate small bowl, beat eggs well. Add eggs to creamed mixture and beat well for 3 minutes, then stir in flour, salt, and baking soda. Divide dough in half. Cool in refrigerator for approximately 30 minutes, then roll out each half of dough separately, about ¼-inch thick. Spread half of the date or raisin mixture on each. Roll dough up; refrigerate overnight. Cut in ⅜-inch pieces and place approximately 1-inch apart on buttered cookie sheet. Bake at 375 degrees for 15–18 minutes or until lightly browned. Leave on cookie sheet for about 5–8 minutes, then remove cookies to a rack to finish cooling.

SNOWBALLS

5⅓ c. sifted all-purpose flour (sifted before measuring)

2½ tsp. salt

2¼ c. shortening or butter, softened

2 c. sifted confectioners' sugar

¼ c. orange juice

4 tsp. vanilla

3 c. pecans or almonds, chopped

Additional confectioners' sugar

Cut together flour, salt, and shortening with pastry blender (not too long) until crumbs are the size of peas. Stir in confectioners' sugar. Add orange juice, vanilla, and chopped nuts; blend well (but don't overmix). Dough should be somewhat crumbly.

Mold dough into 1-inch balls. Place an inch apart on ungreased cookie sheet. Bake at 375 degrees for 12–15 minutes or until bottoms of cookies are lightly browned. Using two spoons, roll cookies in sifted confectioners' sugar while still hot. If sugar soaks in, roll balls in sugar again while still warm.

Prepare prunes by rinsing in scalding water, then wash in cold water. Place in cooking vessel, cover with water, and bring to a simmer. Do not boil.

APPLE SNITZ SNACK

Peel 5 apples and cut into slices. Place on cooling rack. Mix a bit of cinnamon and sugar together; spoon on each apple slice. Bake at lowest oven setting—approximately 150 degrees—for approximately 8 hours or more. While baking, make sure a tray is beneath the rack to catch drippings. For a chewier snack, bake for less time. For a crispier snack, leave in oven longer. If apples get too hard, soften by putting in a bag with soft bread.

Peanut Blossoms

5¼ c. flour	1½ c. peanut butter
1 Tbsp. baking soda	3 eggs
1½ tsp. salt	6 Tbsp. milk
1½ c. butter, softened	1 Tbsp. vanilla
1½ c. sugar	Sugar
1½ c. brown sugar	120 Hershey's Kisses (approx.)

Sift flour, baking soda, and salt together; set aside. Cream together butter and sugars. Stir in peanut butter, eggs, milk, and vanilla; mix well. Stir in dry ingredients. Shape dough into small balls—approx. 1- to 1½-inch—and roll in sugar. Place on ungreased cookie sheet. Bake at 375 degrees for 10 to 12 minutes. Cookies should be slightly browned when done. While cookies are baking, remove wrappers from Hershey's Kisses. As soon as cookies are removed from oven, place a Kiss in the center of each. Allow cookies to cool completely before storing. Layer alternately.

Now therefore hearken unto me, O ye children: for blessed are they that keep my ways. —PROVERBS 8:32

Peanut Butter Balls

8 oz. cream cheese, softened	4 c. powdered sugar
½ c. butter, softened	Melted chocolate
2 c. peanut butter	

Mix cream cheese, butter, and peanut butter together by hand. Gradually stir in powdered sugar; mix well. Form into balls and refrigerate overnight. Dip chilled balls in melted chocolate.

PEANUT BUTTER FUDGE

In heavy saucepan, mix together 2 c. sugar, $^2/_3$ c. milk, and a piece of butter the size of a walnut. Stir over low heat until butter and sugar are melted; then boil briskly until mixture forms a soft ball when dropped in cold water. Remove pan from stove and stir in 2 Tbsp. peanut butter and 2 Tbsp. marshmallow whip. Stir until creamy and pour into buttered pan. Do not beat, as mixture will get hard.

Thou shalt call, and I will answer thee: thou wilt have a desire to the work of thine hands. —JOB 14:15

TAFFY

1 Tbsp. unflavored gelatin	2 c. light corn syrup
$^1/_2$ c. cold water	Vanilla extract
2 lbs. granulated sugar	Paraffin wax (size of a wal-
2 c. cream	nut)

Soak gelatin in cold water. Boil sugar, cream, corn syrup, vanilla extract, and paraffin wax for 15 minutes; stir in gelatin and boil until a tiny bit of the mixture put in cold water hardens immediately (hard-ball test). Let cool. Pull taffy in a cool place, buttering hands slightly so taffy will not stick to them.

Note from Bev

Lots of fun to make and to eat. A quaint and happy Christmas tradition may await you, just as many Amish folk enjoy this family activity during the holidays and beyond.

POPCORN OR PEANUT BALLS

2 c. brown sugar

1 c. light or dark corn syrup

1 c. water

$^{1}/_{4}$ c. butter

Pinch of salt

Popped corn or peanuts

Blend together the sugar, corn syrup, water, butter, and a pinch of salt until sugar is completely dissolved. Continue cooking until the syrup comes together in a soft ball shape. Pour hot syrup over popped corn or peanuts. Shape mixture into balls, buttering your hands first.

MACAROONS

$^{1}/_{2}$ c. sweetened condensed
   milk

2 c. shredded coconut

Vanilla (optional)

Mix together sweetened condensed milk and coconut. Add vanilla if desired. Drop on buttered baking sheet and bake at 350 degrees for 10 minutes.

CRYSTAL STICKS

3 eggs, well beaten

1 c. sugar

1 c. chopped nuts

1 c. chopped dates

1 c. flour

1 tsp. baking powder

Powdered sugar

Mix all ingredients together and spread in a greased shallow pan. Bake at 350 degrees for 20–30 minutes. Cool, cut in strips, and sprinkle with powdered sugar.

Note from Bev

Aunt Ada Reba Bachman was so kind to share this delectable recipe with me, from her childhood memories of growing up at 217 South Queen Street. Her mother, my grandmother Ada, for whom my aunt was named, first created this delicacy for family to enjoy on special occasions.

CANDIED DATES

Slit seedless dates lengthwise. Put smooth peanut butter down inside the dates, plumping them out a bit, enough to widen the dates slightly. Then roll the dates in granulated sugar.

OATMEAL–PEANUT BUTTER–CAROB "FUDGIES"

3 rounded c. quick oats

2 tsp. vanilla

1/2 c. peanut butter

2 c. raw sugar

1/2 c. carob powder (sift after measuring)

1/3 c. olive oil

2/3 c. milk*

Cut oatmeal, vanilla, and peanut butter together with a pastry blender; set aside. Mix together raw sugar, carob powder, olive oil, and milk in a saucepan and bring to a boil over medium heat. Continue cooking at a full boil on medium heat for 2 minutes. Remove from heat and immediately add oatmeal mixture. Mix well and quickly drop by large spoonfuls onto waxed paper. (If mixture starts drying out, it may be heated a bit on low heat, stirring constantly.) Allow "fudgies" to cool for approximately 30 minutes. Makes about 2 dozen.

*Fudgies get especially creamy if raw goat's milk is used.

For the Lord God is a sun and shield: the Lord will give grace and glory: no good thing will he withhold from them that walk uprightly. —PSALM 84:11

Jellies, Jams, Relishes, and Preserves

Hurriedly, she opened the door leading downstairs to the cold cellar. Here, with the help of women from her church district, she'd put up and stored eight hundred quarts of produce. She, in turn, had assisted her neighbors with their canning, as well. Piles of potatoes, onions, turnips, and sweet potatoes were stored separately, more than enough until the next harvest. There were rows and rows of canning jars filled with pickled beets, chow-chow, tomato relish, bean salads, and Rebecca's luscious jams and jellies.

—from *The Shunning*

(Note: see CHOW-CHOW on page 179.)

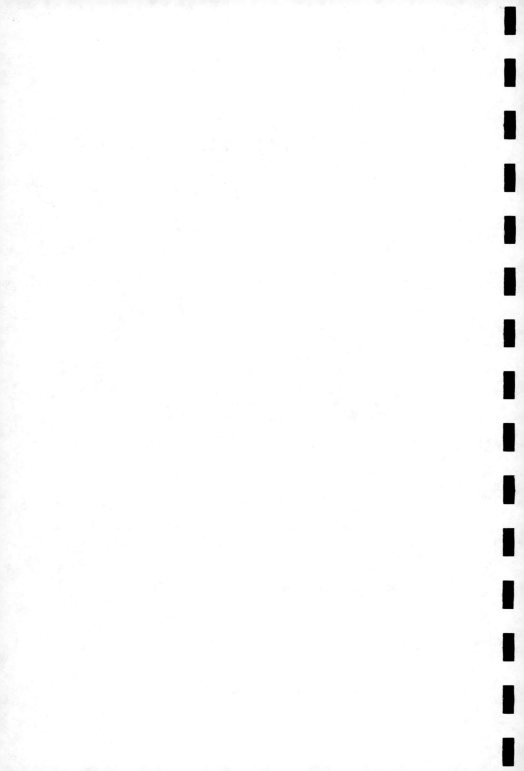

HOT PEPPER JELLY

2 c. peppers*, finely grated   ¼ cup vinegar
3 c. sugar (raw is fine)   1 pkg. Sure-Jell

Drain peppers, then heat for 5 minutes, stirring constantly. Add sugar and vinegar. Heat to boiling; add Sure-Jell. Let boil for 1 minute, stirring constantly. Immediately put mixture in canning jars. Invert jars for 5 minutes. As the jars cool, you should hear each one pop as it seals.

*Use a combination of regular and hot peppers, as desired. Use rubber gloves when handling hot peppers.

Note: One 5-gallon bucket of regular peppers, grated, equals 14 cups. Add 6 cups of grated hot peppers for a total of 20 cups, which makes 10 batches. This recipe may be made in large quantity, but keep the mixture boiling, stirring constantly, while filling the canning jars. If only a small amount is made, it will keep well in a glass jar in the refrigerator without canning.

He which soweth sparingly shall reap also sparingly; and he which soweth bountifully shall reap also bountifully.

—2 CORINTHIANS 9:6

ADAH PEACHEY'S RHUBARB JAM

5 c. rhubarb, chopped   1 3-oz. box red Jell-O (straw-
3 c. sugar   berry, raspberry, cherry,
1 c. crushed pineapple   etc.)

Mix together rhubarb, sugar, and crushed pineapple; let stand for 2 hours. Boil mixture for 10 minutes or until mushy. Remove from heat and add Jell-O. Mix well and put into jars to cool. After jam is cooled, put jars in the freezer.

APPLE, PEACH, OR PEAR BUTTER

Apple Butter:

6 three-gallon buckets of
  apples

20 gallons sweet apple cider
  (or fresh)

20 lbs. sugar

Peach or Pear Butter:

3 three-gallon buckets of
  peaches or pears

12 gallons water

20 lbs. sugar

Apple Butter: Core and quarter the apples. Place in a large kettle and add the cider; cover and simmer on low for 45 minutes or until soft, stirring frequently.

Press cooked apples through a sieve. Discard the skins, return the pulp to the pan, and stir in the sugar.

Simmer, stirring frequently, until the mixture is thick—about 1½ hours. (Or pour the mixture into a roasting pan and bake un-covered at 350 degrees for 1 hour, stirring occasionally. Reduce the oven to 250 degrees and bake 2–3 hours longer, or until thick.)

Sterilize pint jars. Remove the apple butter from the heat and ladle into hot sterilized pint jars, leaving ¼-inch of space from the top. Use a rubber spatula to release air bubbles inside the jar. Be careful to wipe the rim of the jar with a clean cloth. Cap each jar according to the manufacturer's instructions. Process for 10 minutes in a boil-ing water bath (consult a cookbook with directions on boiling bath canning).

Peach or Pear Butter: Follow the instructions above, substituting peaches or pears for apples and substituting water for cider.

Note from Bev

My memories of church picnics and large family get-togethers are filled with apple butter. As a girl, I liked to spread it on toast, on crackers, and even on celery sticks.

PINEAPPLE PRESERVES

3 fresh pineapples   3 lbs. granulated sugar
1 qt. water

Core pineapples; grate either by hand or using a food processor. In a large saucepan, bring water and sugar to a boil. Add grated pineapple and continue to boil another 20 minutes, stirring frequently. When mixture is thick enough, pour into sterilized jars and seal.

Note from Bev

An exceptionally scrumptious jelly.

QUINCE HONEY

1$\frac{1}{2}$ lbs. sugar   2 c. water
1 c. ground quince

Mix together all ingredients and cook for 5 minutes, stirring occasionally. Pour mixture into jars and seal. (Follow home-canning procedures.)

CATSUP

$\frac{1}{2}$ bushel tomatoes   1 c. sugar
$\frac{1}{2}$ c. vinegar   1 Tbsp. cinnamon
$\frac{1}{3}$ c. salt $\frac{1}{2}$ Tbsp. pepper

Boil tomatoes with the skins on, then rub them through a window screen. Add remaining ingredients; let simmer for 45 minutes.

For the wisdom of this world is foolishness with God.

—I CORINTHIANS 3:19

HOMEMADE MAYONNAISE

1 c. cream	1 egg
3 Tbsp. sugar	2 or 3 Tbsp. yellow mustard
1 tsp. salt	1 pt. Miracle Whip
1 rounded Tbsp. real butter	

Heat cream in top of a double boiler. Add sugar, salt, and butter. Beat egg until thoroughly mixed but not frothy; stir into mixture very slowly. Stir continually until custard-like. Strain any lumps. Cool, then mix in mustard and Miracle Whip. Makes approximately 1 quart of extra-rich mayonnaise.

SANDWICH SPREAD

1 gallon green tomatoes (cut in fourths)	3 cups sugar
	3 Tbsp. salt
4 yellow peppers	3 Tbsp. cornstarch
4 red peppers	1½ c. mustard
6 onions	1 qt. salad dressing or mayon-
1 pt. sweet pickles, drained and ground (1 c. juice reserved)	naise

Grind together green tomatoes, peppers, and onions. Add juice from sweet pickles, sugar, and salt; boil together for 20 minutes. Dissolve cornstarch in a small amount of water, enough to make a smooth (not heavy) paste. Stir cornstarch paste into tomato mixture; reduce heat. Add ground sweet pickles, mustard, and salad dressing; heat through but do not boil. Can according to home-canning procedures.

Cantaloupe is delicious eaten with pepper.

Aunt Lizzie's Tartar Sauce

3/4 c. mayonnaise (homemade
    is best; see recipe on page
    176)
1/2 tsp. minced onion
1 tsp. chopped sweet pickle

1 tsp. chopped green olives
1 Tbsp. minced parsley
2 tsp. minced capers
1 Tbsp. tarragon vinegar

Fold vegetables into mayonnaise. Add vinegar; chill. Serve with any type of fish.

The light of the eyes rejoiceth the heart: and a good report maketh the bones fat.   —PROVERBS 15:30

Corn Relish

5 pts. corn (cooked and cut
    off cob)
5 pts. cabbage, chopped
5 red peppers, seeded and
    chopped

2 qts. vinegar
1 1/2 lbs. sugar
2 Tbsp. salt
1/4 lb. mustard seed

Place all ingredients in a large kettle and boil for 30 minutes. Pour into sterilized canning jars and seal hot.

Note: If unfamiliar with the canning process, a good resource is the *Ball Blue Book of Preserving* (available by calling 1-800-392-2575, option 1).

Note from Bev

This mouth-watering recipe from Grandmother Ada's recipe files makes oodles of succulent relish.

CRANBERRY RELISH

1 20-oz. can crushed pinepple

1 pt. fresh or frozen cranberries

2 oranges, peeled and diced

1 large apple, diced

Honey or sugar

Drain pineapple, reserving and setting aside juice. Mix cranberries, oranges, apple, and pineapple together; chill. Stir in reserved pineapple juice; sweeten to taste with honey or sugar.

She looketh well to the ways of her household, and eateth not the bread of idleness.   —PROVERBS 31:27

GREEN TOMATO MINCEMEAT

2 lbs. fresh green tomatoes,
chopped

2 tsp. salt

1 c. suet

1/2 c. water

4 lb. sugar

3 c. chopped apples

3 lb. raisins

1 lemon, seeds and stem
removed, ground

Grated peel of 1 orange

2 tsp. cinnamon

2 tsp. nutmeg

1 tsp. cloves (optional)

1/3 c. vinegar

Sprinkle salt over tomatoes; let stand 1 hour. Drain, discarding juice. Cover tomatoes with cold water; boil for 5 minutes. Drain, add suet and 1/2 c. water; simmer for 20 minutes. Stir in sugar until dissolved. Add remaining ingredients and boil until thick. Put in jars and seal.

Timely good deeds are nicer than afterthoughts.

CHOW-CHOW

6 peppers (red and green)

1 qt. small onions, chopped

1/2 head of cauliflower, broken into florets

2 qts. waxed beans

2 qts. young beans (waxed, lima, and green beans)

2 qts. sweet corn kernels

1 bunch of celery

1 horseradish root, grated

1 oz. celery seed

2 qts. carrots, chopped

1/2 head of cabbage, chopped in 1-inch strips

13 small cucumbers, sliced

1/2 qt. lima beans

2 oz. ground mustard

2 oz. turmeric

2 qt. apple cider vinegar

1 1/4 lbs. sugar

1 Tbsp. cornstarch

Sprinkle of salt

In a large kettle, combine all ingredients; bring to a boil. Cook for 5–7 minutes longer or until vegetables are tender. Pack the mixture into canning jars (washed in dishwasher) and follow home-canning procedures.

Note: If unfamiliar with the canning process, a good resource is the *Ball Blue Book of Preserving* (available by calling 1-800-392-2575, option 1).

Note from Bev

Chow-Chow is a staple of any Amish meal.

PICKLED PEARS

6 qts. fresh pears

6 c. cider vinegar

6 c. sugar

Peel, core, and slice pears; place in kettle. Add vinegar and sugar; cook until tender. Remove pears from liquid and place in sterilized canning jars. Continue to boil syrup until it is nice and thick, then pour over pears and seal jars.

Butter and honey shall he eat. —ISAIAH 7:15

PICKLED CANTALOUPE

2 lbs. cantaloupe   1 lb. sugar
1/2 tsp. pulverized alum   Cinnamon
1 pt. vinegar   Cloves

Peel and seed cantaloupe; cut in 1 1/2-inch square pieces. Boil cantaloupe pieces and alum in water for 10 minutes; drain. Add vinegar, sugar, and cinnamon and cloves to taste. Boil together and place in sterilized canning jars. Seal, following home-canning procedures.

Pickles taste better if allowed to stand at least six weeks before serving.

HANNAH'S DILL PICKLES

4 qts. medium cucumbers   1 qt. vinegar
8 sprays of dill   1 c. salt
4 garlic cloves   3 qt. water

On the day before preparing, wash cucumbers and cover with water. Let stand overnight. The next day, put 1 dill spray in bottom of each of 4 quart jars. Pack cucumbers into jars, being careful not to bruise. Add 1 garlic clove to each jar. Place 1 dill spray on top of each jar. Combine vinegar, salt, and water; bring to a rolling boil. Fill jars to overflowing with vinegar mixture; seal.

Note from Bev

My mother says I loved dill pickles so much that as a young girl, I actually drank the juice at the end of the jar.

Mary Ruth's Piccalilli

2 qts. green tomatoes

2 qts. ripe tomatoes

3 onions

3 red peppers

3 green peppers

1 large cucumber

2 bunches of celery

$^1/_2$ c. salt

Put all vegetables through a food chopper. Sprinkle with salt and let stand in refrigerator for 12 or more hours. Drain well and add the following:

3 pts. vinegar

2 lbs. brown sugar

1 scant tsp. pepper

1 tsp. mustard

Simmer for 1 hour and then pour into hot sterilized canning jars; follow home-canning procedures. (The juice can be drained off and canned for soup, as well.)

Pickled Red Beets and Red Beet Eggs

32-oz. can red beets,
  undrained

1 c. sugar

$^3/_4$ c. vinegar

$^1/_8$ tsp. salt

12 hard-boiled eggs, peeled

In saucepan, mix red beets and juice, sugar, vinegar, and salt. Bring to a boil.

Pour over whole eggs. Allow to cool to room temperature; place in refrigerator for at least 24 hours.

Note from Bev

Very Lancaster County! One of the "seven sweets and seven sours."

Love not the world, neither the things that are in the world.

—I JOHN 2:15

The secret to enjoying life is to be thankful for what each day brings.

BREAD AND BUTTER PICKLES

24 medium cucumbers,
  washed and thinly sliced
10 medium-sized onions,
  finely chopped
1 Tbsp. salt
6 red peppers, seeded,
  chopped, and stems
  removed

1 qt. vinegar
2 c. brown sugar
1 tsp. celery seed
1 tsp. mustard
½ tsp. ginger
1 tsp. turmeric

Mix cucumbers together with chopped onions, salt, and red peppers. Let stand at least one hour. Boil vinegar, sugar, and spices. Add cucumber mixture and bring to almost a rolling boil, stirring frequently with wooden spoon. Pack pickles into hot sterilized jars and seal.

Note from Bev

Another one of Grandmother Ada's time-tested recipes. These pickles are especially good on sandwiches or hamburgers. The whole house will smell of this down-home aroma.

CANNED PEACHES

½ bushel peaches = approx.
  12 quarts canned
1½ c. honey

4½ c. sugar (raw or turbinado sugar work well)
12 c. water

Follow home-canning procedures for canning peaches. (If you are unfamiliar with the procedure, the *Ball Blue Book of Preserving*, available by calling 1-800-392-2575, option 1, has clear instructions.)

Combine honey, sugar, and water and bring to a boil to form syrup; keep syrup simmering while adding to peaches in jars.

Note: Syrup will not be as clear when using honey and raw or turbinado sugar, but it is delicious.

Note from Bev

Canning peaches was a family affair in the busy Buchwalter kitchen—among the daughters, at least. My mother's job was to thoroughly wash all the canning jars. She also remembers the process of tenderly placing each halved peach into the jar, round side out, to make the jars look "pretty." An art form, to be sure.

My meat is to do the will of him that sent me, and to finish his work.

         —JOHN 4:34

Recipe Index

(Alphabetical by Category)